"There is no complete protection against an atomic bomb attack. But there is a lot we can do to reduce the number of deaths and injuries and to check panic. We must organize ourselves in every city, factory, office, and home. Civil defense is a responsibility which begins with the individual. It begins with you. It is shared with the city, the State, and the Nation."

President Harry Truman

"The history of this planet, and particularly the history of the 20th century, is sufficient to remind us of the possibilities of an irrational attack, a miscalculation, an accidental war . . . which cannot be either foreseen or deterred. It is on this basis that civil defense can be readily justifiable—as insurance for the civilian population in case of an enemy miscalculation."

President John F. Kennedy

ATOMIC
WARNINGS

CIVIL DEFENSE PUBLICATIONS
IN THE EARLY COLD WAR, 1945-1965

MICHAEL SCHEIBACH

Name: Michael Scheibach

Title: Atomic Warnings:

Civil Defense Publications in the Early Cold War, 1945-1965

Subjects: Atomic bomb — Civil defense — Atomic Age — Cold War
Postwar — American society — United States

ISBN (Print) 978-1-300-39337-5

CONTENTS

INTRODUCTION

President Harry Truman made the announcement at 7 p.m., Eastern War Time, on August 14, 1945. Truman, who had been thrust into the Oval Office only four months earlier with the death of President Franklin Roosevelt on April 12, told the nation that he had received Japan's unconditional surrender from Emperor Hirohito. World War II had ended.

Truman had not known of the Manhattan Project, the secret government project to build the atomic bomb, when he assumed the presidency. On April 25, Secretary of War Harry Stimson finally told him about a new weapon being developed but did not provide details. Truman later noted in his diary: "We have discovered the most terrible bomb in the history of the world."

The war in Europe ended on May 8 with the surrender of Germany and death of Adolph Hitler. The war in the Pacific against Japan, however, continued, with the Japanese refusing to surrender despite the Allies' overwhelming strength. Military leaders, in fact, were already planning Operation Downfall, the final assault on the Japanese homeland with one million casualties projected.

On July 17, as the Manhattan Project neared completion of the first atomic bomb, President Truman met with British Prime Minister Winston Churchill and Soviet General Secretary Joseph Stalin in Potsdam, Germany, inside the Soviet occupation zone. While attending the conference, Truman received word that the first test of the bomb, the Trinity Test, had been successful.

The United States and Great Britain had given Japan an ultimatum to surrender unconditionally or face total destruction. With no response, Truman gave his approval to use the atomic bomb. When asked for his decision, he wrote: "Suggestion approved. Release when ready."

A specially-equipped B-29 named the *Enola Gay* dropped the first atomic bomb on Hiroshima, Japan, at 8 a.m. on August 6, 1945. The bomb killed some 80,000 people immediately and more than 100,000 people died over the course of the next year from injuries from the blast and the effects of radioactive fallout.

With no response from the Japanese, on August 9 the United States dropped a second atomic bomb on Nagasaki, killing 40,000 people from the blast and thousands more from injuries and radioactive fallout over the next several months.

President Truman's objective—to bring the war to a close—had been achieved with Japan's surrender on August 14. But it came at a high cost.

Almost immediately, radio broadcasts, newspapers, magazines, and books made their main topic "The Bomb" and its political, social, and military impact on the nation and the world.

The Atom Bomb!, published by Independent Book Associates in 1945, announced on its cover: "Here is the Full Story of Atom Power, Present, Past and Future. Is It a Blessing, or Will It Smash Humanity?"

The publication provided an overview of the development of the atom and the atomic bombings of Hiroshima and Nagasaki. It also discussed the atom's positive potential:

"Although Uranium 235 may be dangerous in the hands of individuals, there is no reason why it could not be used, with adequate safeguards, by municipalities and states."

It went on to say in a more foreboding tone: "But the atom is catapulting us into a new epoch. . . . Recognizing that not only the well-being of mankind—but its very existence—is at stake in the control of atom power."

For the next two decades, the federal government; national, regional, and local organizations and associations; state and local civil defense agencies; major corporations; and small businesses published and distributed literally millions of pamphlets, booklets, posters, and books describing the destructiveness of the atomic bomb and presenting instructions on the necessary steps to ensure survival from an atomic attack. Examples of these publications appear on the following pages.

THE BOMB UNLEASHED, 1945-1950

Shortly after the United States dropped two atomic bombs on Japan in August 1945, Rev. W.D. Herrstrom, listed as a "World Traveler, Prophetic Analyst," published *The Atomic Bomb and the End of the World*. Herrstrom adopted the tone of the Old Testament when describing the bomb's destructiveness:

"A sudden blinding flash of light sprays its dazzling brilliancy over a radius of two hundred miles. . . . Like a living monster crawling out of the pit of Perdition, the shadowy figure rocks and reels as it rises to a height of ten miles. . . . What was once a sizeable city is now only a yawning crater with gaping jaws mutely testifying to its voracious appetite for human blood."

In December 1945, Human Events, Inc., Publishers introduced a series of monthly pamphlets focusing on foreign and domestic issues, with the first one by Robert M. Hutchins, chancellor of the University of Chicago, titled *The Atomic Bomb Versus Civilization*. Hutchins argued that the unleashing of atomic energy threatened not only the future of humankind but the future of Earth.

"There is only one subject of really fundamental importance at the present moment," Hutchins wrote, "and that is the atomic bomb. Although it is not a cheerful subject, we must consider it, for the issue is that of survival, to which all other issues are secondary. . . . In fifty years we shall probably be able to start a chain reaction that will blow up the globe."

The following year, 1946, McGraw-Hill Book Company published *One World or None: A Report to the Public on the Full Meaning of the Atomic Bomb*, edited by Dexter Masters and Katherine Way. The publication featured short

The Human Events
● PAMPHLET
for December 1945

● THE ATOMIC BOMB
VERSUS
CIVILIZATION
BY
ROBERT M.
HUTCHINS

20c

essays by the leading figures in the development of the atomic bomb, including J.R. Oppenheimer, Albert Einstein, Harold Urey, and Leo Szilard, as well as commentary by author Walter Lippmann and the Federation of American Scientists.

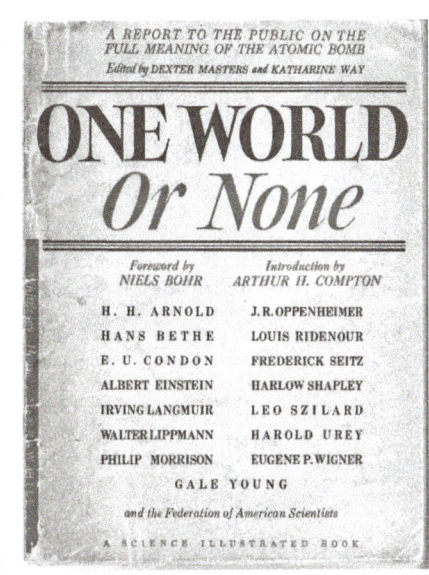

Published less than a year after Hiroshima and Nagasaki, the Federation of American Scientists warned, "The arms race must be stopped. . . . Time is short. And survival is at stake." Albert Einstein, who sparked the Manhattan Project with his 1939 letter to President Franklin Roosevelt warning about Germany's possible development of an atomic bomb, also argued against the bomb's proliferation.

"The construction of the atom bomb," Einstein wrote, "has brought about the effect that all the people living in cities are threatened. Everywhere and constantly, with sudden destruction. . . . [T]he task confronting us requires of all concerned the utmost sagacity and tolerance, which can be achieved only through awareness of the harsh necessity we have to face."

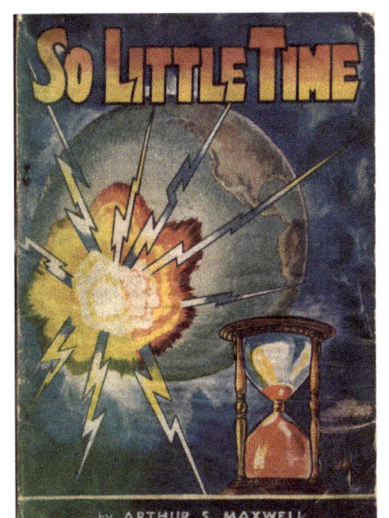

Arthur Maxwell's *So Little Time*, published in 1946, also concluded that the atomic bomb threatened all of humankind. Maxwell, editor of *Sign of the Times*, cited biblical references, writing: "No literal ark awaits to protect us from the coming storm. No ark like Noah's could withstand its fury. We must find our refuge in God. The Most High must be our habitation. Let us make Him our refuge now. . . . There is *so little time*."

The United States was still the only nation in the world with an atomic bomb in 1946, but as these publications warned, it was only a matter of time before other nations became armed with atomic weapons.

This warning became a reality on August 29, 1949, when the Soviet Union successfully exploded its first atomic bomb. Four years after the United States opened the Atomic Age, and still in the early stages of the Cold War with the Soviet Union, the atomic arms race had begun. And the threat of an atomic war escalated.

In 1950, the National Security Resources Board published its first major publication designed to inform and educate the American people about a potential attack by the Soviet Union yet reassure them at the same time that they could survive.

Titled *Survival Under Atomic Attack*, the booklet presented a rather distorted idyllic view of the survivors of the Hiroshima and Nagasaki bombings: "Today thousands of survivors of these two atomic attacks live in new houses built right where their old ones once stood. The war may have changed their way of life, but they are not riddled with cancer. Their children are normal. Those who were temporarily unable to have children because of the radiation now are having children again."

The booklet failed to mention that 80,000 men, women, and children were killed instantly in Hiroshima and 40,000 more in Nagasaki; and that thousands of deaths occurred over the next few years from radioactive fallout and injuries from the blast.

Most civil defense publications, however, focused on the deadly realities of the atomic bomb. By 1950, most states had established civil defense offices and began publishing pamphlets on the dangers of atomic warfare and the necessary steps to ensure survival.

Three civil defense offices in upstate New York joined together in 1950 to publish *If the Niagara Frontier Is Bombed: What to Do In Case of Atomic Attack*. Lucius D. Clay, chairman of the New York State Civil Defense Commission, wrote the Foreword, emphasizing the primary message that

survival is possible if people know what to do:

"There is no COMPLETE defense against an atomic bomb, but, by careful CIVIL DEFENSE planning, NOW, and by full understanding on your part of what you can do NOW and what you should do in time of disaster, the effects of the bomb can be greatly minimized. . . . What you should do in time of attack are simple things—but ALL-IMPORTANT."

The Civil Defense Agency of the Common-

wealth of Massachusetts published *Protection from the Atomic Bomb*, using illustrations to help emphasize its message (see following pages).

A letter from John Stokes, director of Massachusetts civil defense, on the opening page read: "We must face the fact that any bombing attack can cause dreadful destruction and loss of life. . . . Understanding what to expect and what to do under atomic bomb attack can greatly increase the chance for survival, and that is the purpose of this booklet."

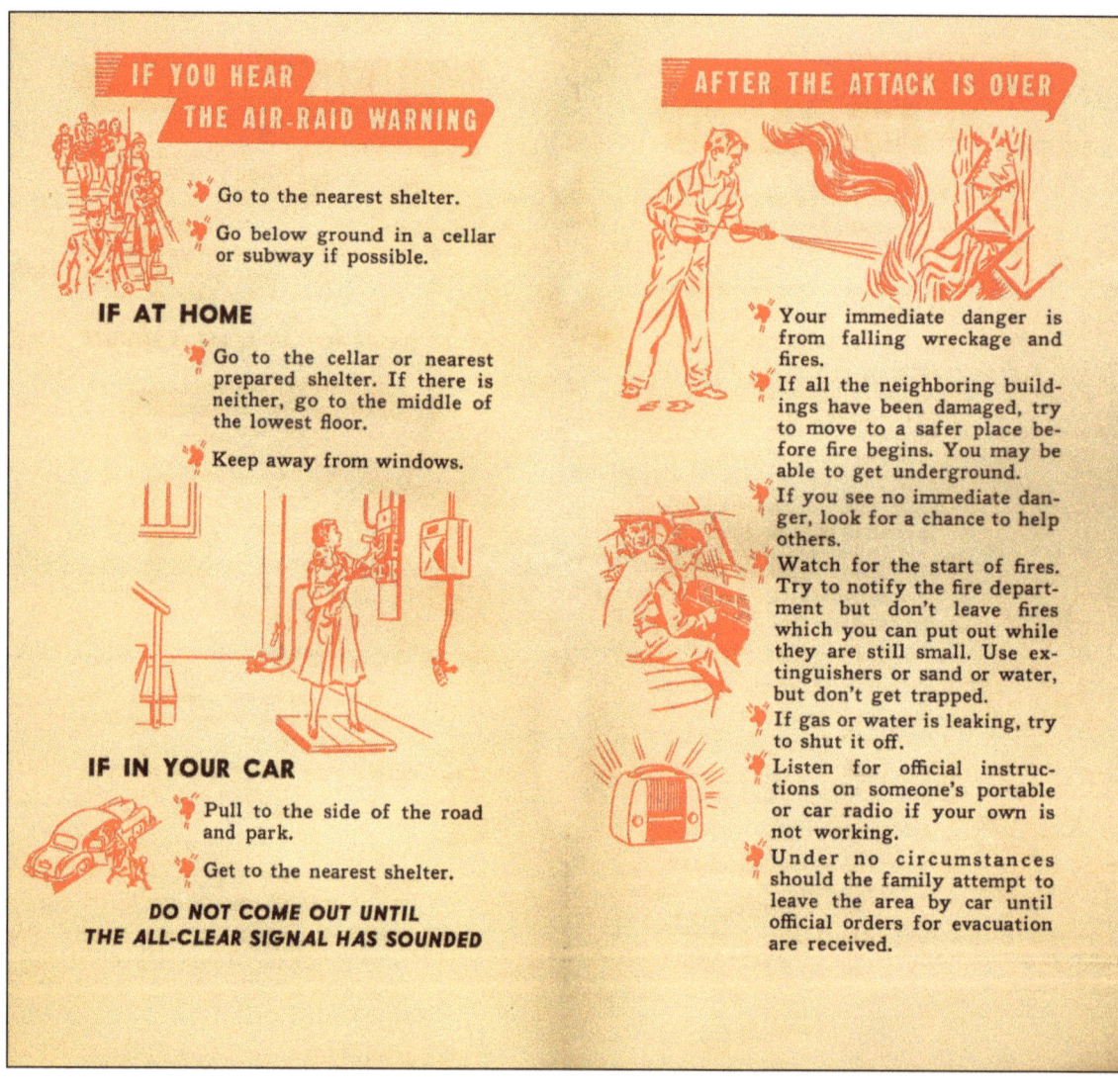

IF YOU HEAR THE AIR-RAID WARNING

- Go to the nearest shelter.
- Go below ground in a cellar or subway if possible.

IF AT HOME

- Go to the cellar or nearest prepared shelter. If there is neither, go to the middle of the lowest floor.
- Keep away from windows.

IF IN YOUR CAR

- Pull to the side of the road and park.
- Get to the nearest shelter.

DO NOT COME OUT UNTIL THE ALL-CLEAR SIGNAL HAS SOUNDED

AFTER THE ATTACK IS OVER

- Your immediate danger is from falling wreckage and fires.
- If all the neighboring buildings have been damaged, try to move to a safer place before fire begins. You may be able to get underground.
- If you see no immediate danger, look for a chance to help others.
- Watch for the start of fires. Try to notify the fire department but don't leave fires which you can put out while they are still small. Use extinguishers or sand or water, but don't get trapped.
- If gas or water is leaking, try to shut it off.
- Listen for official instructions on someone's portable or car radio if your own is not working.
- Under no circumstances should the family attempt to leave the area by car until official orders for evacuation are received.

Illustration from *Protection from the Atomic Bomb*.

IF YOU HAVE HAD NO WARNING IN AN A-BOMB ATTACK

WHEN YOU SEE A FLASH OF LIGHT BRIGHTER THAN THE SUN —

- Don't run: there isn't time.
- Fall flat on your face.
- **GET DOWN FAST!**

IF IN-DOORS

- GET DOWN!
- Drop to the floor to avoid flying window glass.
- Crawl under or behind something.
- Cover up.

STAY DOWN FOR AT LEAST ONE MINUTE

IF OUT-OF-DOORS

- GET DOWN!
- Drop to the ground: close against a wall if possible.
- Cover up.
- Stay down until the blast has passed; then get under the heaviest cover nearby.

STAY THERE FOR AT LEAST A MINUTE

IF IN YOUR CAR

- Stop the car fast, set the emergency brake, and dive for the floor.

STAY DOWN FOR AT LEAST A MINUTE

IF YOU HAVE NO AIR-RAID WARNING

WHEN YOU SEE THE FLASH THERE IS NO TIME TO RUN

WHEREVER YOU ARE GET DOWN FAST

Illustration from *Protection from the Atomic Bomb*.

13

The New York State Civil Defense Commission published *You and the Atomic Bomb: What to Do In Case of an Atomic Attack* in 1950, distributing thousands of copies throughout the state. The pamphlet described the destructive power of the atomic bomb from an air burst, a ground burst, and a water burst.

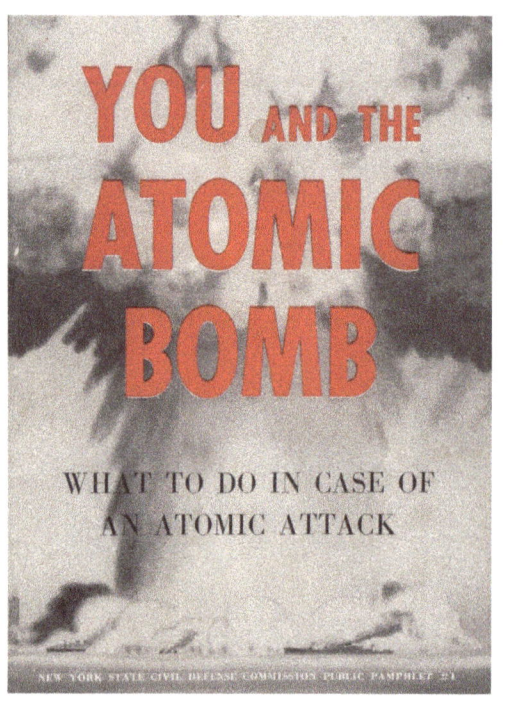

"We hope that your closest acquaintance with an atomic bomb will be in reading this pamphlet," it began. "But if you are to understand what to do if an A-bomb should fall on your city, you must first know what an A-bomb does."

It also included information about radiation, fire, first aid, and what to do in an air raid, especially a sneak attack: "In case of a sneak attack there are several things you can do to protect yourself, even though you may not be able to reach shelter.

"The blinding flash of the explosion will be your first warning. If you are in the open, immediately fall to the ground face down next to a building wall, if possible, so you will be shielded from falling brick and stones. Close your eyes and cover your face, neck and arms. This will give you some protection against the deadly radiation and scorching heat.

"If you are on the street, dodge into a doorway if it is not more than a step or two away. Stand to one side under the arch of the door. Turn away from the flash and cover your face and other exposed areas of the body.

"If you are in the house, crawl under a bed or table or drop behind a sofa or other large object which can protect you from flying glass. Keep out of line with windows. *Cover up.*"

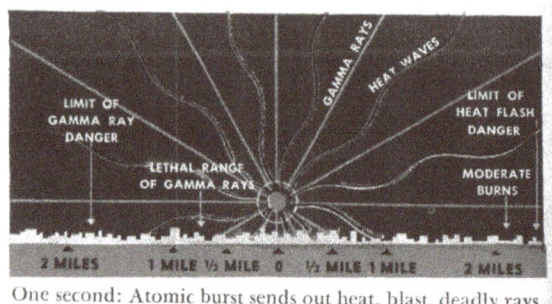

One second: Atomic burst sends out heat, blast, deadly rays.

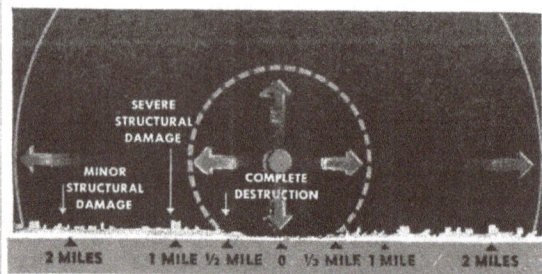

10 seconds: Immediate effects are over. Damage indicated.

Johnny says...
Knowledge is Your Best Defense!

IF YOUR CITY IS ATTACKED
KNOW WHAT TO DO!

WHEN YOU HEAR A 3 MINUTE WAILING SIREN

1. Get off the street. Park car at curb.
2. Head for a building or other shelter.
3. Indoors, go to a shelter, basement or inside hall.
4. Keep away from windows.
5. Don't use food or water in open containers.

JOIN NOW!

IN SNEAK ATTACK... *without warning*

1. Outdoors, get under cover. Fall flat.
2. Indoors, get under a bed or table.
3. Cover exposed skin. Close eyes.

LAWRENCE WILKINSON • LT. GEN. CLARENCE R. HUEBNER
CHAIRMAN   DIRECTOR
New York State Civil Defense Commission.

CIVIL DEFENSE
CD
NEW YORK

PRESENTED AS A PUBLIC SERVICE BY
PHILIP MORRIS CIGARETTE CO.

Philip Moris issued this sign in support of New York City's civil defense efforts.

The Glenn L. Martin Company, an aircraft manufacturing company in Middle River, Maryland, north of Baltimore, published *What to Do If an Atomic Bomb Strikes* as a service to its employees. It was later reprinted by the *Baltimore Sun* for the general public.

As with most pamphlets published in 1950 or earlier, this one provided factual information about the atomic bomb from the impact of the initial blast to the lingering effects of radiation.

"Protection from the effects of radioactive contamination presents a problem that has not previously been encountered. The results of blast and fire are visible and can generally be controlled in a relatively short period following an explosion. But nuclear radiation cannot be detected by the senses without the use of instruments, and unless the contamination is removed, the deleterious effects may continue for weeks, months, or longer."

The booklet detailed the effects of radiation and the critical steps to minimize them, but it also attempted to ease fears that an atomic bomb might trigger worldwide contamination of radioactivity.

"If the whole surface of the earth is to be contaminated, with a minimum number of bombs," the booklet read, "they would have to be exploded within a short period of time. Further, since contamination from fission products would be due essentially to the fallout, sufficient time must be allowed for all

First-aid centers should be in blast and fire resistant buildings and should not be so located that inflammable structures are adjacent.

the particles to settle out. On the basis of these possibilities, it has been calculated that in order to constitute a worldwide hazard, something like a million atomic bombs, of the nominal size, would have to be detonated, roughly one to each 200 square miles of the earth's surface. This clearly is improbable."

Treatment of Burns

For practical purposes of diagnosis and treatment, it is not necessary to dis-

Falling hair will be one of the results of exposure to an atomic blast. The effect will not be permanent, however, and the hair will grow back with little or no change.

tinguish among burns caused by thermal radiation, by flame, or by contact. Although there are differences with respect to extent of body surface involved, depth of the injury to the skin, and general reactions of the individual to burns of different types, the indicated treatment for burns due to an atomic explosion appears to be the same as for those encountered in large-scale incendiary raids and in civil disasters.

BRIEF GUIDE TO THE
ATOMIC AGE

Richard M. Fagley

In *Brief Guide to the Atomic* Age, divergent views of the future were offered by Richard M. Fagley, a member of the Federal Council of Churches of Christ of America.

"The possibilities of the Atomic Age for both good and evil surpass imagination," Fagley wrote. "It would be nice to dream about the constructive possibilities; but unfortunately, until atomic power is made safe for mankind, the benefits will not amount to much. The main value in thinking about them is to strengthen our determination to choose life instead of death for ourselves and humanity.

"How can this weapon of destruction be controlled so that it may become a tool of industrial progress? How can we make atomic power a blessing instead of a curse? That is the problem we face, government leaders and ordinary citizens alike. It is the biggest single social issue we face in the postwar world.

"Right now the only known factories for making atomic bombs are in the United States. For the moment there can hardly be war, since no country or combination of countries without the bomb could take on one country possessing it.

"But how long can we keep exclusive control? . . . How long can we keep the secret to ourselves? . . .

"The fact that the bombs are so destructive would not prevent war, but would push nations into aggression. As Norman Cousins has pointed out in the *Saturday Review of Literature*, the more deadly the weapon, the more likely the outbreak of war."

As the Cold War intensified in the late 1940s, the nation's educators also responded. A new objective emerged: preparing America's youth for the Atomic Age—both its opportunities and its dangers. The National Association of Secondary-School Principals, a department of the National Education Association, introduced *Operation Atomic Vision* in 1948 for senior high schools.

The learning unit, designed to emphasize the positive side of atomic energy, was prepared by Hubert Evans, associate professor of science, and Ryland Crary, assistant professor of history, at Columbia University in New York City; and C. Glen Hass of the Denver, Colorado, Public High Schools.

The unit provided an overview of four essential aspects of the atomic-bomb: The New World A-Coming; The Hazards of the New World; What Are We Doing With Atomic Energy?; and Your Stake and Your Job in Operation Atomic Vision, which explained its purpose:

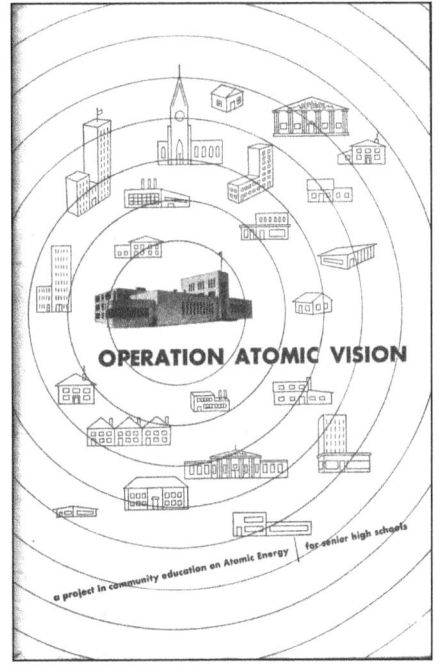

"Atomic Energy? What do you think of when you hear these words? The chances are that these words call up in your mind thoughts of war, destruction, the atomic bomb. This is not strange for, after all, the press and radio and many prominent people have emphasized the great hazard of war and the A-bomb. Perhaps the words, "atomic energy," strike fear in your heart and cause you to dread a recurrence of the awful destruction at Hiroshima. You may even wish to bury your head in the sand and resign yourself to fate.

"But there is a much brighter, a much more constructive, and a much more thrilling side to the atomic energy picture. If we look long enough and hard enough at this side of the picture, we might be able to see a world free from war, strife, poverty, and sickness; a world of hope and of great possibilities for human welfare.

"This is what Operation Atomic Vision is about—the two sides of the atomic picture with the bright side always in the center of attention. It is not too much to believe that atomic energy can be controlled and directed toward the building of a new world. But it won't happen automatically. There is learning to be done; there is straight thinking to be done; there is work to be done by all."

The National Securities Resources Board published *The Atom and You* in 1950. The 64-page booklet covered all aspects of the atomic bomb, including the blast, burns, radiation sickness, and the difference between ground and air bursts. It also provided instructions on household safety, first aid, and fires. One chapter focused specifically on food and water, which would be essential in an atomic attack:

"To prevent harm from accidentally eating or drinking radioactivity, throw out all unpackaged foods that were lying around where dust from ground bursts or mist from underwater bursts might have settled on them. And before opening canned or bottled goods, wash the outside of the containers thoroughly. That will remove most of the pollution that may have gotten on them.

"Also be sure that all cooking utensils and tableware are scrubbed clean in order to remove any invisible radioactive dusts. Food and utensils that were in closed drawers or tight cupboards will be all right. If it was an air burst, don't worry about the food in the home. It will be safe to use.

"Be careful drinking water after atomic explosions. There is little or no chance that water actually inside household pipes at the time of attack will be made radioactive. If a little is drawn off right after the burst and placed in clean containers with covers, it should tide you over the immediate post-raid period. But even if the water continues running, don't keep using tap water for drinking purposes unless you have received official information that the city system is safe. This is not only because of radioactivity, but because of other dangers like typhoid that can come from damaged water systems."

Scrub well to remove radioactive particles from the skin.

Move an injured man only if the location is dangerous. Otherwise give first aid and wait for the doctor.

YOUR CHANCE TO SURVIVE

½ Mile from the Bomb—

1 Chance out of 10

1 Mile from the Bomb—

5 Chances out of 10

1 ½ Miles from the Bomb—

9 Chances out of 10

From *The Atom Bomb and You.*

KILL THE MYTHS

ATOMIC WEAPONS WILL NOT DESTROY THE EARTH

Atomic bombs hold more death and destruction than man ever before has wrapped up in a single package, but their over-all power still has very definite limits. Not even hydrogen bombs will blow the earth apart or kill us all by radioactivity.

DOUBLING BOMB POWER DOES NOT DOUBLE DESTRUCTION

Modern A-bombs can cause heavy damage 2 miles away, but doubling their power would extend that range only to $2\frac{1}{2}$ miles. To stretch the damage range from 2 to 4 miles would require a weapon more than *8 times* the rated power of present models.

RADIOACTIVITY IS NOT THE BOMB'S GREATEST THREAT

In most atom raids, blast and heat are by far the greatest dangers that people must face. Radioactivity alone would account for only a small percentage of all human deaths and injuries, except in underground or underwater explosions.

RADIATION SICKNESS IS NOT ALWAYS FATAL

In small amounts, radioactivity seldom is harmful. Even when serious radiation sickness follows a heavy dosage, there is still a good chance for recovery.

From *The Atom Bomb and You.*

What to Do . . . You and the Atomic Bomb, published in 1950 by the Portland (Oregon) Bureau of Disaster Relief and Civil Defense, provided five specific steps to prepare in advance for an atomic attack:

"1. LEARN ALL YOU CAN ABOUT THE BOMB. The atomic bomb is a tremendously powerful weapon—but it is not all powerful. Its principal effects of blast—and its secondary effects of heat and radiation—are definitely limited in their scope.

"2. PREPARE A SHELTER OR REFUGE ROOM. Equip it with emergency toilet and fire-fighting equipment and first aid materials. If for a family or residential group, stock it with extra clothing, canned water, and emergency food supplies sufficient to sustain the family or group for five days. *Do not hoard.*

"3. PREPARE FOR FIRE by cleaning all rubbish out of the garage, attic, and basement. Make your house and contents as fireproof as possible—*and keep them that way.*

"4. COOPERATE WITH YOUR BLOCK WARDEN. His mission is to keep you informed of developments in civil defense—to coordinate rescue, first aid, and firefighting activities within the block—and to call for help when the facilities of the block cannot cope with the situation.

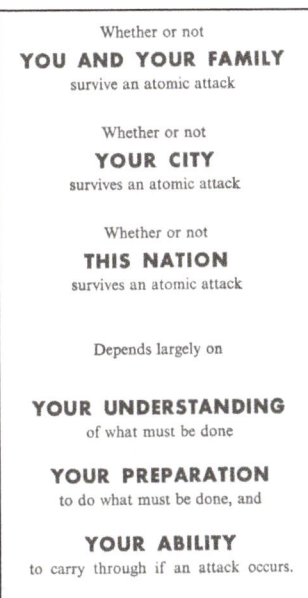

Whether or not
YOU AND YOUR FAMILY
survive an atomic attack

Whether or not
YOUR CITY
survives an atomic attack

Whether or not
THIS NATION
survives an atomic attack

Depends largely on

YOUR UNDERSTANDING
of what must be done

YOUR PREPARATION
to do what must be done, and

YOUR ABILITY
to carry through if an attack occurs.

"5 LEARN THE AIR RAID WARNING SIGNAL. The air raid warning . . . is a series of blasts on air horns located throughout the city. One five-second blast is sounded daily at 12 noon for test purposes. Learn this sound. The immediate danger signal is a series of three short blasts repeated continuously for three minutes. The all-clear signal is three one-minute blasts."

"If an atomic attack occurs without warning, however, you must cover your eyes with your arm and drop to the floor, if you are at home or in a building; drop to the ground, if you are outside; and, if in a car, truck, or taxi, stop the vehicle, put it in park, cover your eyes, and get down as low as possible.

23

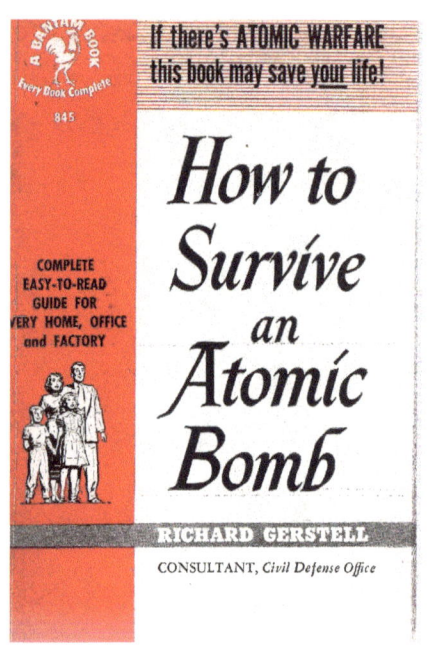

How to Survive an Atomic Bomb

RICHARD GERSTELL

CONSULTANT, *Civil Defense Office*

In 1950, Richard Gerstell, a consultant with the National Security Resources Board, published *How to Survive an Atomic Bomb*. One of the most comprehensive books in the early Cold War, it contained information about the atomic bomb and practical and thorough steps to take in order to survive an atomic blast. The introduction, titled "Please Read This First," read:

"An atomic bomb may never drop on this country. That's what we all hope. But we can't be sure of it. If an atomic attack does come, this book may save your life.

"No book can help much if you're close to the middle of an atomic explosion and in the open. But if you're alive a few seconds after an atomic bomb goes off—and the odds that you will be alive are all in your favor—this book will keep you from further risking your life. . . .

"Everything in this book applies to modern atomic bombs. If far more powerful bombs are invented, the figures in this book will change somewhat, but the advice about what to do will be much the same.

"If you want a better chance of living through an atomic attack—if you want your family to have a better chance—then read this book. And see that your whole family understands it, too."

Gerstell's practical advice was for men and women to wear hats and long-sleeved shirts or blouses, and for women outdoors to wear stockings, which would

If you are caught outdoors in a sudden attack, a hat will give you at least some protection from the heat flash.

not protect them from "prompt rays" but would help guard against flash burns.

Despite the serious instructions on how to survive an atomic bomb, popular culture and the advertising world found plenty of humor in the bomb as shown in the cartoon at right.

ATOMIC BIG SHOT

HEY, JERK--YOU'RE NOT ATOMIC!

ALL YOU DO IS RAVE AND BOIL!

BUT I'LL ADMIT--YOU'RE JET-PROPELLED

WHEN YOU TAKE ····CASTOR OIL !!!

ATOMIC AWARENESS, 1951-1953

On January 12, 1951, nearly eighteen months after the Soviet Union exploded its first atomic bomb, President Harry Truman signed the Federal Civil Defense Act of 1950. The Act gave the president the authority to prepare the American people for a possible atomic attack as well as to take the necessary steps to respond if such an attack were to take place.

The Act had four sections: Organization; Powers and Duties; Emergency Authority; and General Provisions. The declaration of public policy provided the general principles on which the Act was to be administered. It read: "It is the policy and intent of Congress to provide a plan of civil defense for the protection of life and property in the United States from attack. It is further declared to be the policy and intent of Congress that this responsibility for civil defense shall be vested primarily in the several States and their political subdivisions. The Federal Government shall provide necessary coordination and guidance; shall be responsible for the operations of the Federal Civil Defense Administration as set forth in this Act; and shall provide necessary assistance as hereinafter authorized."

In his statement, President Truman said, "This master plan, entitled 'United States Civil Defense,' is now serving as a blueprint for American states and cities in their preparations to safeguard American lives and homes. The federal government can and will provide the necessary coordination and guidance for the civil defense program."

The FCDA was to be headed by an administrator appointed by the president with the advice and consent of the Senate. The Federal Civil Defense Act also created a Civil Defense Advisory Council consisting of a chairman and twelve members to advise and consult with the FCDA administrator on matters related to civil defense.

Truman chose Millard Caldwell, former governor of Florida, for administrator, and he served until November 1952. Jerry Wadsworth replaced Caldwell as an interim administrator because of Dwight Eisenhower winning the 1952 presidential election. President Eisenhower then named Val Peterson, governor of Nebraska, as the FCDA head.

The FCDA became the primary government agency for the nation's civil defense, including the creation of volunteer programs in police service, nursing service, communications, fire service, health service, welfare service, transportation, rescue service, and warden service. It conducted training, held conferences, produced films, and published informational, educational, and instructional materials.

Among the first pamphlets published by the FCDA was *The Warden's Handbook*, which began by complimenting and encouraging the new warden volunteers:

"Since pioneer days, Americans have joined together to combat common dangers of warfare and natural disasters. Again we are faced with a serious threat—a threat that an enemy attack may destroy our homes, kill our people, and paralyze the productive power of our cities. You, the block warden, have joined other civil defense volunteers to meet this threat. Progress in civil defense recruiting, equipping, and training is being made throughout the country. If this progress continues and we become strong enough, an enemy will think twice before he attacks."

The Warden's Handbook provided detailed information on the block warden unit—fire, rescue, first aid, evacuation, and communications—with emphasis on the various steps before and after an attack:

"Before an attack, the unit must record and maintain information about residents, available protective equipment, and physical features of the block; and organize and train block residents and neighborhood groups on how to protect themselves.

"When the public warning is sounded, people should be directed to shelters. Dimouts and blackouts, if ordered, must be enforced. Disabled, ill, and otherwise incapacitated persons must be warned and, if necessary, assisted to shelter. Calmness, efficiency, and assuredness on your part and on the part of each member of your unit will do much toward the prevention of panic.

"After an attack, the unit must mobilize the resources of the block to perform first aid, extinguish small fires, and conduct rescue efforts. It also needs to report casualties, damage, and general conditions, as well as direct people to reception centers and emergency welfare centers, where they would be able to find food, clothing, and temporary lodging."

The handbook ended by reminding the warden that his or her job did not end after an attack. Rather, it was just beginning. "You must be ready."

"The strength and courage of American women—traditional guardians of the home—is one of the nation's greatest resources. If the women of this country will prepare with courage and determination, we will have the Civil Defense we need to be strong." So concluded the first annual report of the Federal Civil Defense Administration in 1951. The

FCDA called for 17 million civil defense volunteers and estimated that at least 60 percent of these would be women. Recruiting women, in fact, became one of the FCDA's primary efforts.

In 1952, it published *Women in Civil Defense*, which began: "The home is the basic unit of the community—and the basic unit on which defense of the home front must be built.

"Whether you are a housewife, secretary, business executive, or nurse, civil defense looks to you, as a woman, to take an active role in protecting your home. No one else can do that job for you."

Much has been written about women returning to the home after their participation in war production during World War II. In fact, the number of women in the labor force did decrease after the war, and working women gravitated toward more gender-traditional jobs, such as teachers, sales, and clerical positions. Yet civil defense offered women in the early postwar era an opportunity to expand their roles both as paid employees in state and local civil defense departments and agencies, and as volunteers in FCDA programs such as the warden service, nursing, auxiliary police, communication, transportation, and administration.

In *Women in Civil Defense*, the FCDA stressed the duty of women to join civil defense. Women had two duties in civil defense. The first was to educate their families about the atomic bomb and the necessary steps to ensure their survival. The second duty was to become actively involved in a community civil defense organization; and, if none existed, to start one.

"If your community does not have an active civil defense organization, much of the blame must fall on you and your neighbors," it read. "Unless you, as a responsible American woman, take action you are gambling with the safety of your family, your friends, your community, and your country.

"You would hardly blame others for failing to provide food, clothing, and shelter for your family. That is your family responsibility. And so is family civil defense. Community civil defense can be effective only if the families of the community are solidly behind it, willing to give time and effort to make it work. National civil defense can be only as effective as the people of the Nation make it. . . .

"When you have trained your family and prepared your home, you have more than doubled your chances for survival in an atomic attack.

"When you have joined in organizing your community, you have given the community and the Nation a far better chance to survive an enemy attack.

"But you will have done more than just prepare in case of war—you will have made a positive contribution to keeping the peace.

"Getting America prepared on the home front is a responsibility that falls in large part on the shoulders of all American women. It's your job—and you have no time to waste."

FAMILY CIVIL DEFENSE

Here are the simple steps you should take now to prepare your home and family against enemy attack:

1. Learn the civil defense air-raid alert signals.
2. Equip the most protected place you can find in or near your home for an air-raid shelter.
3. Learn the effects of an atomic explosion and the safety precautions you can take at home or at work to minimize danger and injury.
4. Prepare an emergency first-aid kit for your home.
5. Take a regular Red Cross first-aid or home nursing course as soon as you can.
6. Practice fire-proof housekeeping. Learn to fight fires in the home.
7. Get official civil defense identification tags for yourself and family, if available.
8. Learn the simple safety measures you and your family must take to protect yourself against germ and gas warfare.
9. Maintain a three-day supply of food and adequate water for use in an emergency.

By 1951, radio stations began offering 32-page manuals prepared by local civil defense organizations and promoted over the air. Listeners of WDGY in Minneapolis-St. Paul, WGN in Chicago, WONS in Hartford, Connecticut, and radio stations nationwide simply had to request the manual. It was then sent to them courtesy of the station, the local civil defense agency, or a corporate sponsor, such as Acme Welding & Engineering Company in Hammond, Indiana, which sponsored the *Chicagoland Civil Defense Manual*.

The manuals contained letters from state and local civil defense officials as well as prominent persons in the community who stressed the need for civil defense. Robert McCormick, editor and publisher of the *Chicago Tribune*, for example, opened the Chicagoland manual by writing, "Protection of people against the A-Bomb is principally a matter of making the best of what you have."

Eric Hoyer, Minneapolis mayor, wrote in his city's manual, "By use of the global bomber in modern warfare, the City of Minneapolis is vulnerable to an attack by any foreign enemy of our nation. . . . Civil defense is the cooperative effort of our citizens for self-protection."

The manuals contained comprehensive information about the national, state, and local civil defense efforts, including drills, air-raid sirens, and medical plans. Training courses were listed as well as the various options for those interested in volunteering, including the Warden Service, Ground Observer Corps, auxiliary police, clerks, nurses, and drivers, to name a few.

The manuals also included a Personal Protection Section with specific information on building bomb shelters, knowing what equipment and supplies are needed, and stocking the shelter with the proper food and water to last at least seven days. In addition, manuals had instructions on what to do if the bomb falls with advance warning and without advance warning.

The Personal Protection Section also contained the various ways the atomic bomb could be detonated: underwater, ground level, and air bursts.

The Chicagoland manual offered a description of the differences between an atomic bomb and a conventional bomb in four ways: "(1) ENERGY released by an atomic bomb is roughly equivalent to that produced by the explosion of 20,000 tons of TNT bombs; (2) the explosion of the bomb produces highly penetrating, invisible RADIATION in the form of lethal gamma rays; (3) intense HEAT (1,000,000 degrees C. in the center of the fireball) and LIGHT (at 5.7 miles, the brilliance is 100 times that of the sun viewed at the earth's surface); and (4) RADIOACTIVE RESIDUES which remain after the explosion emitting harmful radiations.

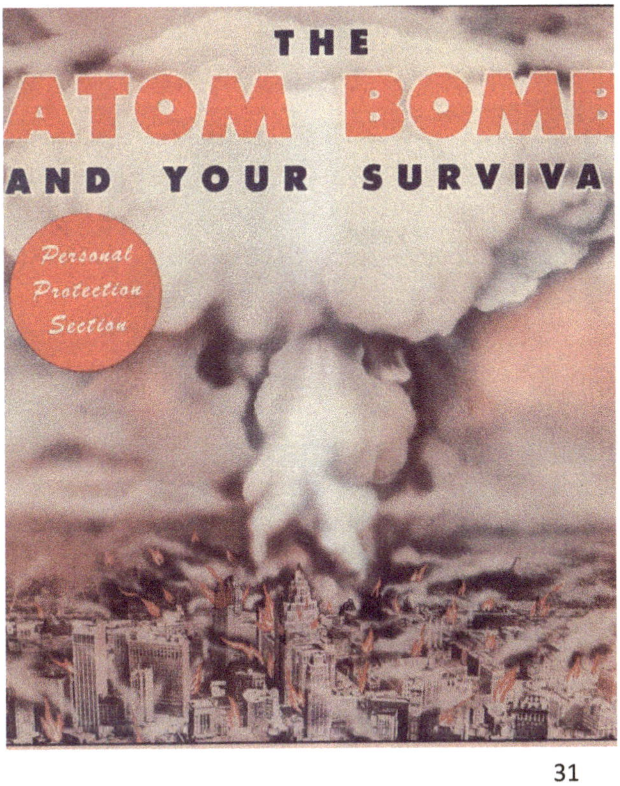

The Chicagoland manual's main message was emphasized in all caps::

AVOID PANIC

BE CALM

MASS HYSTERIA CAN SERIOUSLY

HAMPER ORGANIZED DEFENSE.

Most civil defense publications in the early 1950s, before the introduction of intercontinental ballistic missiles (ICBMs), included illustrations such as the one below showing the projected path of Soviet bombers equipped with atomic bombs. Many also featured Air Raid Instructions (right).

OBEY these official Civil Defense

 **AIR RAID** *instructions*

| AIR-RAID ALERT *(immediate attack)* | 3 minute wailing siren or short blasts |
| ALL-CLEAR *(attack over)* | 3 one minute blasts 2 minutes silence between |

Quickly but Calmly	*with* **NO WARNING**	*with* **WARNING**
at **HOME**	Drop to floor. Get under bed or heavy table.	Go to prepared shelter. Turn off all appliances.
at **WORK**	Drop to floor. Get under desk or work bench.	Obey Wardens. Go to assigned shelter.
at **SCHOOL**	Drop to floor out of line of windows. Bury face in arms.	Obey your teacher. Go to assigned shelter quietly.
in the **OPEN**	Drop to ground or dive for cover. Bury face in arms.	Obey Wardens. Go to nearest OK'd building or shelter.
in **VEHICLES**	Drop to floor. Bury face in arms.	Get out. Go to nearest OK'd building or shelter.

stay put until the all-clear and obey instructions

The escalation of the Cold War, with increasing concerns about a possible atomic attack by the Soviet Union, led states across the country to establish civil defense departments and cities to form local civil defense offices. Between 1951 and 1953, scores of civil defense pamphlets were distributed by these offices with warnings about the atomic bomb and instructions on the steps to take to ensure one's survival.

The Denver, Colorado, Civil Defense Office published *Just In Case Atom Bombs Fall* in 1951, with Quigg Newton, mayor of Denver, introducing the publication with this message: "We do not expect Denver to be bombed. But no one can assure us that war will not occur, or that in war, Denver will not be bombed. The only safe course is to be prepared. The best weapon of civil defense is knowledge, because knowledge is power to survive."

Also included was a letter from George Berger, Jr., director of the city's Civil Defense Office.

"Defense and offense both are now dependent on survival and activity of each civilian," Berger wrote. "Production of war material can mean the difference between defeat or victory more than ever before in the history of the world. Civilian populations, representing a nation's power to produce material goods now are as much in the front-lines of warfare as the fighting troops.

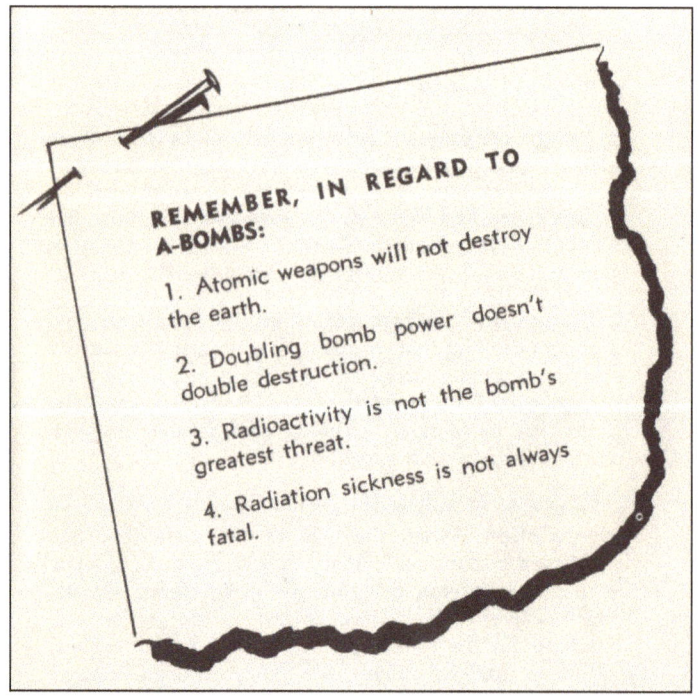

REMEMBER, IN REGARD TO A-BOMBS:

1. Atomic weapons will not destroy the earth.

2. Doubling bomb power doesn't double destruction.

3. Radioactivity is not the bomb's greatest threat.

4. Radiation sickness is not always fatal.

"The individual in America today must regard self-preservation as a duty not only to himself but to his nation."

The pamphlet went on to provide illustrated instructions on what to do before an attack, during an attack, and after attack, as well as how to cope with radiation sickness.

WHAT TO DO BEFORE THE ATTACK

1. KNOW YOUR OWN HOME, or the apartment house or hotel where you live. Know how to get to those parts of your residence that will probably afford you the greatest protection from a bombing. Generally speaking, well-constructed basements afford this protection (but be sure two exits exist, so that you can still get out if one is blocked). You are usually safer against a wall away from the center of the building, because there is less danger here from falling beams. Know where you keep  your first-aid materials, fire-extinguishing devices, and extra quantities of food. Have flashlights handy.

2. STRIVE FOR FIREPROOF HOUSEKEEPING. Don't let trash pile up. Keep waste paper in covered containers. Store paints and other inflammable liquids carefully. All parts of your house should be readily accessible, particularly the attic. Remove furniture, boxes, magazines, rags and other inflammable mate-

premises ARE damaged, turn off gas at the meter if you can do so safely. IMPORTANT: once the gas valve at the meter is turned off, do not turn it on again yourself—call for a trained man. If you smell gas, extinguish all open flames. Do not strike matches. Open doors and windows and get outside the building. Close fuel and draft doors on coal furnaces.

3. KEEP FLASHLIGHT HANDY. Don't strike matches because of the danger of blasts from leaking gas mains.

4. SHUT OFF VENTILATING FANS unless they are equipped with special filters to keep out radioactive dusts.

5. KEEP PETS INDOORS. Pets can bring in radioactive dusts.

6. REMOVE YOUR CAR from the streets if you have ample warning. Leave streets open for emergency travel. Roll up car windows to keep out radioactive dust. DO NOT JUMP IN YOUR CAR in an effort to leave the city. You would be caught in slow-moving traffic. YOU WILL BE MUCH SAFER AT HOME.

rials from the attic. Distribute buckets of water or sand through your house if bombing attacks appear imminent. A shovel, heavy gloves, and a garden hose adapted to inside faucets would all come in handy for controlling fires.

IF YOU ARE AT HOME, and you hear the warning of an impending air attack, STAY AT HOME.

1. SHUT DOORS AND WINDOWS and pull down shades; this will help keep out fire sparks and radioactive dust. Shutters or venetian blinds, or heavy drapes, help protect you from flying glass.

2. WHEN AN ALERT SOUNDS, turn off your gas range burners and all other hand-operated gas appliances. Do all you can to eliminate sparks by shutting off the furnace. DO NOT turn off gas at the meter. DO NOT turn off your pilot lights. Turn off non-automatic gas appliances, such as manually-operated water heaters or room heaters. If your premises are NOT damaged by the attack, DO NOT USE GAS except for emergency purposes. If your

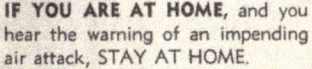

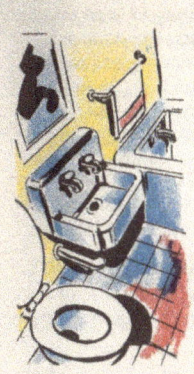

7. BE CAREFUL OF WATER. A little water left standing in the pipes at the time of blast can be used. Wait for instructions on further use of water. Boiling water will not remove radioactivity, but will kill germs that might have gotten in through breaks in the mains.

8. DON'T TAKE CHANCES WITH FOOD in open containers. To prevent radioactive poisoning or disease, select your food with care. Stick to canned and bottled foods if possible.

9. IF NEAR THE BOMBED AREA, throw out unpackaged foods lying where dust might have settled on them. Wash outside of cans or bottles thoroughly before opening. Be sure utensils and tableware are clean. Food and utensils in closed drawers or tight cupboards will be safe to use.

10. SCRUB ALL CONTAMINATED OBJECTS in buckets or tubs used for that purpose only.

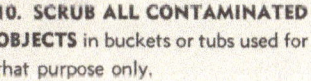

IF YOU HAVE ONLY A SECOND'S WARNING

1. FALL FLAT ON YOUR FACE. This greatly lessens chances of blast injury; also of flash burns. More than half of all wounds result from being tossed about or from being struck by falling and flying objects.

2. IF YOU'RE IN A BUILDING. Flatten out close against the cellar wall; or any inside wall; or under a bed or table. Don't pick spot opposite windows because of flying glass.

3. IF OUTDOORS—Fall face-down against the base of a good substantial building; or a handy ditch or gutter. Don't look up; hold face in arms 10 or 12 seconds after blast to prevent burns and temporary blindness.

4. TO PREVENT FLASH BURNS. Try to find shelter, such as a high wall, high bank, or some solid object; if further away, even light cotton cloth will help.

Illustration from *Just in Case Atom Bombs Fall*.

DURING A BOMBING ATTACK

1. KEEP COOL. Avoid chaos; prevent disorder and havoc.

2. STAY HOME. That is the safest place. If you are away from home, get under cover in the nearest shelter; avoid crowded places; stay off the streets; the enemy wants you to run out into the streets and create a panic.

3. LIE DOWN. This is the most important single thing you can do. Try to find protection. In buildings keep away from the center of the floor, where danger of falling beams is much greater. You are also safer near a structural column of a building. Outside, keep away from trees or flimsy structures. Curl up to protect face, neck and arms from flash burns.

4. AFTER EXPLOSION, keep away from radioactive dust. Keep home closed. Change clothes. Take a shower. Remember, water safe for bathing purposes may not be safe for

Illustration from *Just in Case Atom Bombs Fall*.

37

AFTER THE BOMBING ATTACK

1. PUT OUT SMALL FIRES. If incendiary bombs fall, play a spray from a garden hose (NOT a splash or stream) on the bomb.

2. GIVE FIRST AID. You will not be hurt by helping a person injured by radioactivity. Radioactivity is not contagious. Wash yourself and your clothing afterwards to get rid of radioactive dust.

3. KEEP ALL GAS APPLIANCES TURNED OFF.

4. DON'T PICK UP ARTICLES contaminated by radioactivity.

5. TAKE A SHOWER—and use lots of soap. Change clothes.

6. DON'T DRINK ANY WATER from other than approved sources. A little left in the pipes can be drawn off for emergency use.

7. DON'T SPREAD RUMORS.

8. IF WATER IS CUT OFF, don't flush toilets until sewer service is restored.

Illustrations from *Just in Case Atom Bombs Fall.*

9. DON'T LAUNDER CONTAMINATED CLOTHES IN WASHING MACHINES. Use a tub especially set aside for this purpose. Undress in basement to avoid contaminating rest of house.

10. IF CLOTHING IS HEAVILY CONTAMINATED, BURY IT.

11. WASH YOUR HAIR THOROUGHLY, for that is one place where radioactive dusts are likely to pile up. Get all dirt from beneath your fingernails. All this is necessary for persons in contact with radioactive materials in heavily contaminated areas.

WHAT ABOUT RADIATION SICKNESS?

The severity of radiation sickness depends upon how strong a dose a person gets. Medical science can treat for overdoses of radioactivity. Half or more of the people made very sick by radioactive causes would recover. Like sunburn, radiation can cause a person to become nauseated. But if you become nauseated after an air attack, don't jump to the conclusion that it is caused by radiation sickness. You might be sick to your stomach for many other reasons.

As the national civil defense program expanded with the creation of the Federal Civil Defense Administration in January 1951, President Truman took the next step by issuing Executive Order 10312 establishing CONELRAD (**Con**trol of **El**ectromagnetic **Rad**iation), the nation's first emergency broadcasting system, on December 10.

At a time before intercontinental ballistic missiles, the military was concerned that Soviet bombers equipped with atomic bombs could use over-the-air radio broadcasts to pinpoint target areas. Allied bombers had done just that during World War II by monitoring German radio stations.

In March 1951, the FCC held an "Informal Government–Industry Technical Conference," which resulted in a document describing how the system, then called Key Station System, would work: "The arrangement requires certain telephone circuits (private wire or direct line to Toll Board) between the Air Defense Control Centers (A.D.C.C.) and specified radio stations to be known as 'Basic Key Stations.' Additional telephone circuits (direct line to Toll Board) will be required in certain cases, between 'Basic Key Stations' and other stations to be known as 'Relay Key Stations.'

Each 'Basic Key Station' receiving an alert or warning signal from the A.D.C.C. shall, if so directed, proceed to broadcast a predetermined message and also relay the message by telephone to all 'Relay Key Stations' under his control as specified."

With CONELRAD, all radio and television stations would leave the air following an alert issued by the Air Defense Command of the U.S. Air Force. The stations would be replaced by CONELRAD, which would broadcast emergency information over 640 or 1240 on the radio dial. People would hear this message:

"We interrupt our normal program to cooperate in security and civil defense measures as required by the United States government. This is a CONELRAD radio alert. Normal broadcasting will now be discontinued for an indefinite period. Civil defense information will be broadcast in most areas at 640 and 1240 on your regular radio receiver."

What would you do if...

enemy bombers *were* to attack our country? How do you find out quickly what is happening and what to do?

Prompt, accurate civil defense information could help save your life, your neighbor's . . . your city.

The CONELRAD system of Public Emergency Broadcasting is one of the surest and fastest ways of getting word to you under attack conditions. If our country is ever attacked, here's *how* and *where* you will get official civil defense news and instructions.

> In a civil defense emergency, remember to use your AM (Standard) Radio. *Tune to 640 or 1240 on your Radio Dial*
> Your AM (Standard) radio will keep you in touch with what is happening.

Your television set and FM (frequency modulation) radio will go off the air in a civil defense emergency, because their broadcasting beams could be used as direction finders by enemy bombers. Use your AM (Standard) radio.

The Veterans of Foreign Wars Post No. 3477 in Athens, Ohio, dedicated its 52-page civil defense booklet titled *It Could Happen Here!* to those who gave their lives in World War I, World War II, and Korea. The booklet began will a plea for civil defense volunteers:

"Civil defense in our town and in the nation is an organized program for the protection of lives and property. It is not a separate municipal or Federal department, but an integral part of the lives of all our citizens. Our Civil Defense efforts have made great progress in the past year. Thousands of volunteers are being trained in first aid, police, and fire duties. Through the Block Organization, our neighborhoods are steadily making progress in preparing themselves for any emergency.

"Doctors, farmers, communication workers, and all groups of labor and industry are organizing for disaster operations. School children are being taught how to protect themselves and the people around them.

"This organizational activity will continue in the months to come until the people of this area are as well or better protected than the citizens of other sections of our nation. To accomplish this goal, however, we must make an indifferent public aware of its responsibility. Each citizen must do his share to protect his town and his nation. It can truly be said that Civil Defense is everybody's business.

"Volunteer for civil defense now."

The booklet described in detail the destructive power of the atomic bomb with illustrations showing the second-by-second impact on a house. It then covered what each home—and each woman in the home—needed to do to prevent fires, as well as what to do to fight a fire if necessary:

"Getting ready to fight fires is a big part of the civil defense job.

"After an atomic bomb explodes, the resulting fires could cause more loss of life and property than the blast itself.

"An atomic bomb would cause great fires in the area where it fell. It also would start hundreds of small fires in surrounding areas. These smaller fires must be fought by people on the spot because the regular fire-fighting companies won't be able to reach them.

"Teaching of householders to fight fires will be carried out by local civil defense instructors. Auxiliary or reserve firemen will be recruited to back up the regular companies. These civil defense volunteers will be trained by local fire companies using regular equipment.

"At least one member of your family must be trained in the use of basic fire-fighting tools and methods." (See illustrations on the following pages.)

The booklet offered eight fire-fighting tips: give your house a "civil defense house-cleaning"; keep plenty of water on hand; make sure your fire-fighting equipment is in good order and readily available; make your family "a fire fighting team"; don't panic if there is a fire; never stop fighting a fire unless your life is in danger; don't enter a burning building alone; and, most important, take civil defense training.

REMOVE
HOME FIRE HAZARDS

Chimney and roof in good condition?

Attic a junk pile?

Stairs or halls cluttered?

Trash and rubbish near your house?

Electrical circuits and fixtures OK?

Paint rags? Shavings near work bench?

Is your basement a fire hazard?

Fuel within 3 ft. of furnace?

Open paint or oil cans?

Piled-up paper and rubbish?

Then . . .

When your house is cleared of fire hazards assemble your fire fighting tools:

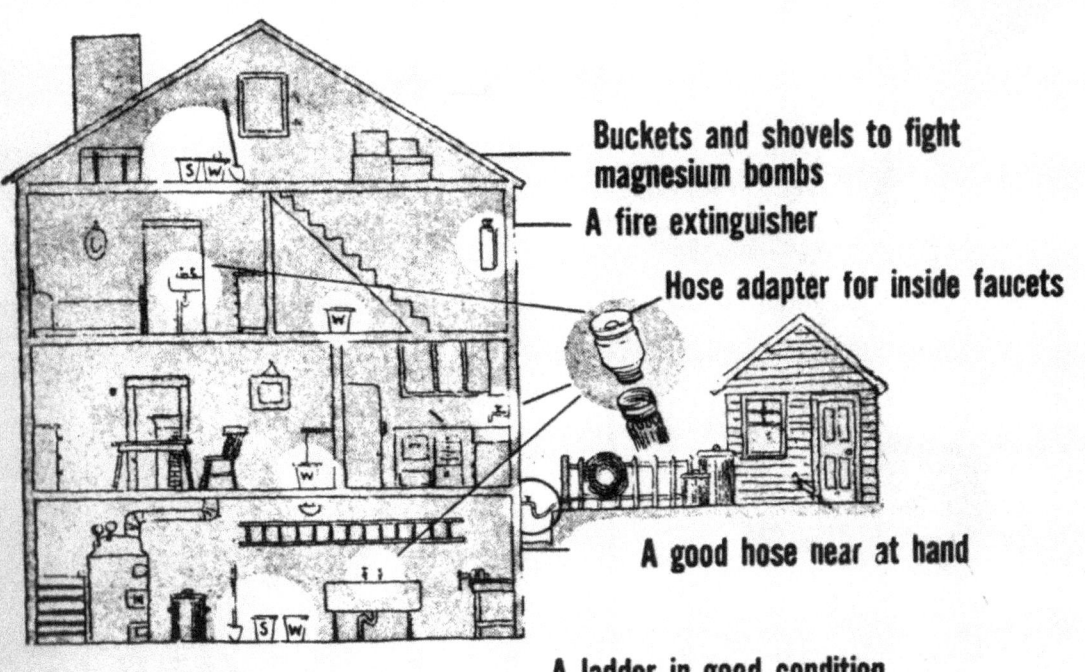

Buckets and shovels to fight magnesium bombs

A fire extinguisher

Hose adapter for inside faucets

A good hose near at hand

A ladder in good condition

Sand and covered water buckets throughout your house

EVACUATION FOR SURVIVAL, 1954-1957

The Cold War escalated in November 1952 with the United States successfully testing a hydrogen bomb, which was a thousand times more powerful than the bombs

dropped on Hiroshima and Nagasaki in August 1945. Less than a year later, in August 1953, the Soviet Union tested its own hydrogen bomb, raising new concerns about the effectiveness of civil defense. Then, in 1957, the Soviet Union successfully tested its first intercontinental ballistic missile (ICBM), which reduced the warning time to a matter of minutes rather than hours.

The FCDA had two missions: first, to inform and instruct the American people about how to survive an attack by the Soviet Union; and, second, to reassure the American people that they could survive.

To enhance its second mission, the FCDA asked Al Capp, the creator of the Lil' Abner comic strip, to create a pleasing and upbeat image to use for the civil defense program. Capp responded with Mr. Civil Defense, which became a common figure in FCDA publications.

With the introduction of the H-bomb, the FCDA's first mission—to instruct the American people on how to survive—shifted its emphasis from seeking shelter to evacuating as quickly as possible. Congress responded to the threat of atomic war by passing the National Interstate and Defense Highways Act of 1956, which established the interstate highway system.

Between 1954 and 1957, civil defense offices across the country, from major metropolitan areas, such as Los Angeles, San Francisco, Seattle, and Atlanta, to moderate-sized cities, such as Milwaukee, Wisconsin, Birmingham, Alabama, and Topeka, Kansas, as well as small towns, published pamphlets with evacuation maps indicating how to move out of the city if given at least two hours' warning before an attack.

WHEN THE BOMB GOES OFF

—don't BE there!

BIRMINGHAM
AND
JEFFERSON COUNTY
CIVIL DEFENSE

Your GUIDE FOR

DEFENS
AGAINS'
THE
H-BOM

WASH.
COUNTY

1955

EVACUATE

DON'T SIT UNDER THE MUSHROOM

SEATTLE & KING COUNTY
DEFENSE DEPARTMENTS

Evacuation
Map
Instruc

PREPARED

DENV

CIVIL DE

OFFI

EVACUATION GUIDE FOR A
CIVIL DEFENSE EMERGENCY

Your
ROUTE to
survival

ATLANTA METROPOLITAN AREA OF CIVIL DEFENSE
Elliott R. Jackson, Director
MUNICIPAL AUDITORIUM   JA. 5-4843

it's
your
LIFE

he San Francisco Plan

ncisco DISASTER COUNCIL AND CORPS

San Francisco 2, California • HEmlock 1-2121, Local 614

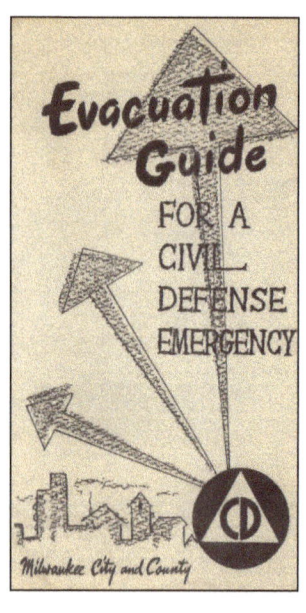

The *Evacuation Guide for a Civil Defense Emergency*, published by the Milwaukee Civil Defense Administration, included a map as well as reassurance that if the city were hit by an atomic bomb, "you can still survive":

"Because of the H-bomb, best measures for safety consist of getting out of the city at least 20 miles, for the farther out you are the better your chances of survival.

"We can be fairly sure of a TWO-HOUR WARNING before an enemy could get here. Even two hours may not be enough time for everyone to get far enough away to save himself. But, the farther away you get, the better your chances. Later on, as the air defense warning system and escape routes improve, you will have more time and better roads to leave the city."

The publication also had recommendations for dealing with radioactive fallout: "When an H-bomb explodes close to the ground, thousands of tons of earth and debris are made radioactive and are sucked upward. The heavy particles fall to earth quickly but the lighter ones are carried away by the wind and fall to earth over a wide area. This fallout is a very dangerous thing. However, winds in this area normally blow from west to east. It is unlikely that you will be caught in a radioactive fallout area any distance from Milwaukee. ...

"Consult your Home Defense Officer about your plan. If father has the car, your plan should include a car pool ride with neighbors. Your Home Defense Officer can help get neighbors together. Civil Defense needs many Home Defense Officers. These are principally women and are being trained daily. You should volunteer for this training. Call your local civil defense office."

The Atlanta (Georgia) Metropolitan Area of Civil Defense published *Your Route to Survival: Evacuation Guide to a Civil Defense Emergency*, with an evacuation map and instructions on how to prepare for and survive an atomic attack. It also contained fourteen points to remember:

"1. The success of this plan depends largely upon your understanding and cooperation.

"2. It can happen here but you can still have time.

"3. The ALERT—EVACUATION SIGNAL is a steady sound on sirens and other devices for 5 minutes—to be repeated 3 times or more. It means ATTACK IS PROBABLY—START EVACUATING.

"4. THE TAKE COVER SIGNAL is a rising and falling wailing sound on the sirens for 3 minutes—repeated over and over. It means ATTACK IS IMMINENT. TAKE THE NEAREST BEST AVAILABLE COVER.

"5. When you hear the ALERT—EVACUATION SIGNAL, turn your radio to 640 or 1240 on your radio dial and listen for further instructions, while preparing yourself and your family for immediate evacuation. Take emergency supply of food, clothing, water, and first aid items.

"6. Study the maps and select the nearest and most accessible evacuation route from WHEREVER YOU AND EACH MEMBER OF YOUR FAMILY ARE WHENEVER THE ALERT—EVACUATION SIGNAL sounds.

"7. Load your vehicle to capacity.

"8. All evacuation routes are ONE WAY OUTWARD. Do not CROSS any of them.

"9. When you get onto an evacuation route, keep moving outward. Do not try to pass another vehicle. Keep calm.

"10. Select a family meeting place so members can get together again.

"11. If you have no car, start walking towards an evacuation route. Someone will pick you up.

"12. Keep your gas tank half full at all times.

"13. DUCK AND COVER if an attack is made without warning.

"14. Obey instructions received over Conelrad and from police and authorized Civil Defense Personnel."

Birmingham, Alabama, published one of the most direct civil defense messages—and best advice—to its population and to those throughout Jefferson County in its pamphlet describing the city's emergency evacuation plan: *When the Bomb Goes Off—Don't Be There!*

The pamphlet included an evacuation map (opposite page) and detailed information and guidance on what to do if an atomic bomb devastated Birmingham:

"IT CAN HAPPEN HERE . . . Our detection system, fighter planes, and anti-aircraft guns and guided missiles are all being made bigger and better. But still, one enemy plane getting through with a modern H-Bomb could destroy or severely damage more than half the Birmingham metropolitan area.

"YOU CAN STILL SURVIVE . . . Because of this powerful weapon, a new Civil Defense plan has been made. Downtown Birmingham probably would be the most likely target due to its heavy population. However, the Fairfield-Ensley industrial area and Bessemer are also prime targets and in all probably would be bombed. When a bomb drops, the further you are from the danger zone the better your chances of survival.

"YOU HAVE TIME . . . Living in the southern part of the United States, we can be fairly sure of a two to four hours' WARNING before the enemy could get here. Even this amount of time may not be enough for everyone to get far enough away to save himself. But one thing is for sure! The farther away we get, the better our chances. Later on, as our continental warning system is improved, we may get 4 to 6 hours . . . enough time for almost all of us to get out of the danger area.

"EVACUATION SIGNALS—HERE'S WHAT YOU DO . . . As soon as you hear the Alert-Evacuation signal on the Air Raid sirens, immediately turn your radio to 640 or 1240 on your dial [CONELRAD]. All radio and TV stations will go off the air . . . Listen for further instructions while you are preparing yourself and your family for immediate evacuation. START MOVING OUT. Stay calm, but START MOVING! If each of us knows what to do and follows directions, we can all move with less trouble and more speed.

"GET OUT TO SAFETY . . . Wherever you are, when you hear the Evacuation Signal on your Air Raid sirens, get out of the danger area the best way that you can. Use your own car if you can get to it. If not, go to your nearest automobile dealer who will furnish you with transportation. . . .

"If you wish, you may hitch a ride with others in any transportation available. In a crisis like this, the automobile will be your best friend. EVERY CAR SHOULD BE FULL. If you cannot find a ride, start walking, as organized public transportation may be able to pick you up enroute. Get as far away from downtown Birmingham as possible—up to forty (40) miles or more if you can. You may be delayed on the way out more than once, but STAY WITH YOUR RIDE, if you have one. Thus, you will still get out faster and farther than by walking. If the car in front of you breaks down or runs out of gasoline, help push if off of the highway and distribute its passengers in other cars. Do not permit delays because of disabled automobiles.

"SUBURBAN AREAS . . . If you live in the areas immediately outside Birmingham—such as Tarrant, Mountain Brook, Homewood, Fairfield, and Bessemer—there are many county and secondary roads that may be used to get you to safety. Select the one NOW that is best suited for evacuation of your family.

"GETTING YOUR FAMILY TOGETHER AGAIN . . . Families should plan now how to get back together again. A good plan is to pick a family meeting place (such as the home of a friend or relative) 15 to 50 miles from Birmingham. Then, after each member of the family gets out of the danger area, he can try to get to this meeting place or at least to get word to it about himself. In this way, it should not take too long to reassemble the family.

"THE DOWNTOWN GET-AWAY AREA . . . Permits traffic to move outward in any direction; all drivers must observe traffic signals and one-way streets. OUTSIDE OF THE DOWNTOWN AREA—All traffic will move in one direction only—Outbound, and will disregard the traffic light signals. Traffic on these escape highways will be controlled by Police, Military, and Civil Defense Personnel."

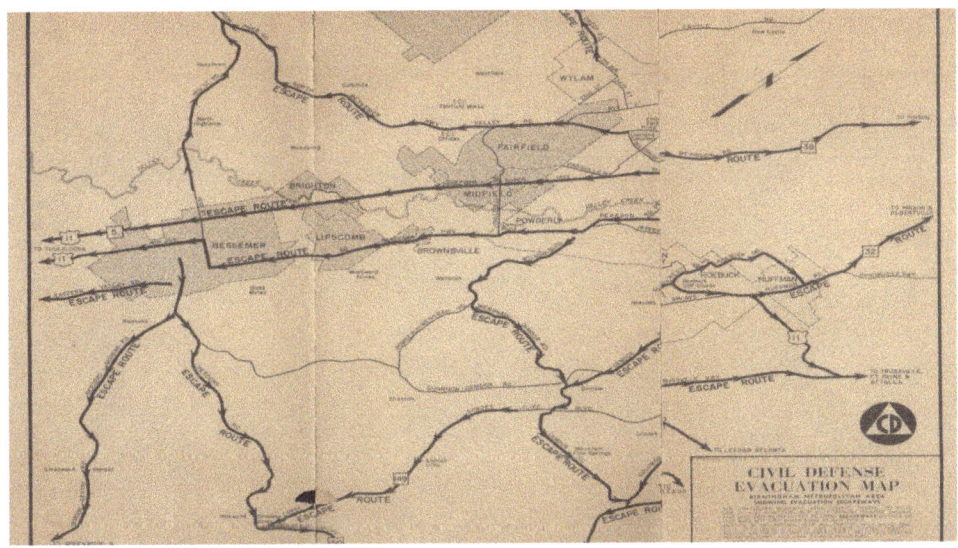

The Seattle and King County Civil Defense Departments titled its evacuation pamphlet *Don't Sit Under the Mushroom*, which stressed that Seattle was considered a major target area for an atomic attack.

"A 10-Megaton Hydrogen Bomb can be dropped on the center of the business district," the pamphlet read. "This would cause utter destruction for a radius of 4 miles, major destruction for a radius of 7 miles, moderate destruction for 10 miles, and minor destruction out to 13 miles.

"This bomb may be dropped any time day or night with or without warning. If practically no warning or very little, the 'Take Cover' signal will be used. If sufficient warning time to justify an attempt to evacuate, the 'Alert' Evacuation Signal (3-minute steady blast) will sound. ACT IMMEDIATELY!

"There will not be time to use our highways for two-direction traffic. In order to take full advantage of our limited evacuation routes and limited time to save as many people as possible, one-way outbound traffic is a requirement. Cross traffic will be impossible.

"The city will be divided at Madison Street. Everyone north of Madison will move north; those south of Madison will move south or east over the floating bridge. This means many families may be separated and going in different directions. The map shows routes, and shaded areas indicate reception areas. Select one as your family reuniting point."

The pamphlet then answered the four essential questions asked most often:

"WHY? A Hydrogen Bomb attack is possible. You must get beyond the 13-mile circle (see map) to be reasonably safe. Prepared shelters rather than evacuation offer the best chance for survival beyond the 13-mile circle.

"WHEN? A steady 3-minute blast, which will be repeated, means Evacuate if you are within 13 miles of center of the City. Start moving. A wailing siren or short blasts mean

Take Cover immediately. Do not confuse them. Tune your radio to the Conelrad frequency (640 or 1240) to verify the signal.

"WHERE? Travel on your proper evacuation route beyond the 13-mile circle and keep going until stopped by traffic control, a blockade, or you reach a Reception Area.

"If blocked by traffic after passing the 13-mile circle, turn off the highway wherever you can. People behind you will still be in the danger area. Your action may mean their lives.

"HOW? By car, truck, bus, rail, or ship. If no transportation available, walk away from the center of the city to where you may be picked up by others.

"In many county areas an average person can walk beyond the 13-mile circle in one to two hours. If along the waterfront and without transportation, check on the possibility of boarding a ship which is capable of getting under way. . . . If you have a car, truck, or bus be sure to pick up a full load.

"Industries, stores, office buildings, neighborhoods, etc., are urged to make local plans so that all available transportation is used and everyone knows where to get transportation.

"Know your local plan."

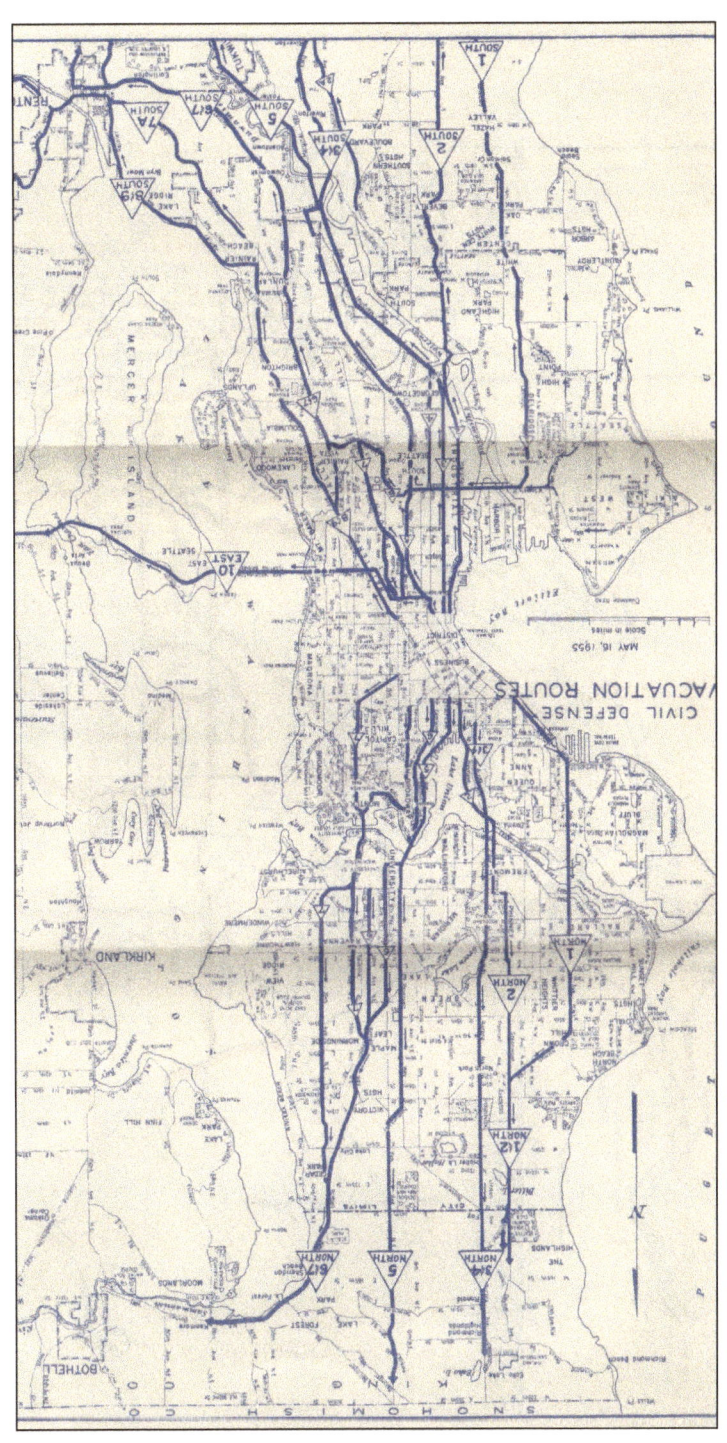

it's your LIFE ... The San Francisco Plan

SAN FRANCISCO DISASTER COUNCIL AND CORPS.
45 Hyde Street, San Francisco 2, California · HEmlock 1-2121, Local 614

"When any disaster comes, self help is essential. Organized aid from authorities civil or military cannot possibly assist each individual immediately. . . . The plan is a simple, common-sense means to survival. It is in complete agreement with, and is coordinated with, State and Federal policy.

"Your survival in disaster depends mainly on you. Now is the time you and your family must inform yourselves, make your decisions, and determine individual action. This is the best way to insure survival."

These were the opening words of *It's Your Life: The San Francisco Plan*, published by the San Francisco Disaster Council and Corps, a comprehensive publication that included an evacuation map (right) as well as reminders about the various warning signals, what supplies to take in a "Ready Pack," how to prepare for an attack, and understanding the danger of radioactive fallout. It also contained vital information for parents concerning their children if they were in school when an attack occurred. The pamphlet included a statement by President Dwight Eisenhower: "Until a stable peace prevails in the world, we must stay strong and vigilant. Thus peace and

TO MOTHERS — AND OTHER PARENTS

If the siren (▒▒▒▒▒▒▒▒) to evacuate is sounded when children are in school, several plans will go into effect. The plan to be followed by the individual child is for the parent to decide. The decision must be made in advance and school authorities notified now, if not already advised.

Plan #1. Children will be evacuated at once by first available transportation. These children will be called for by their families later at reception area.

Plan #2. Children will await parents or neighbors to evacuate them. *After a reasonable wait, children not called for will be evacuated by school authorities.*

Plan #3. Children whose parents wish them to remain in the City, will be taken to shelter in the school or nearby. There, they may remain if joined by a parent or designated adult. *After a reasonable wait, unaccompanied children will be evacuated by school authorities.*

preparedness are joined. Our Civil Defense program is essential to both. An effective Civil Defense is an important deterrent against attack on our country and thus helps preserve peace. . . . Should an emergency occur, our nation's survival may be dependent upon the way each of us responds to his duty."

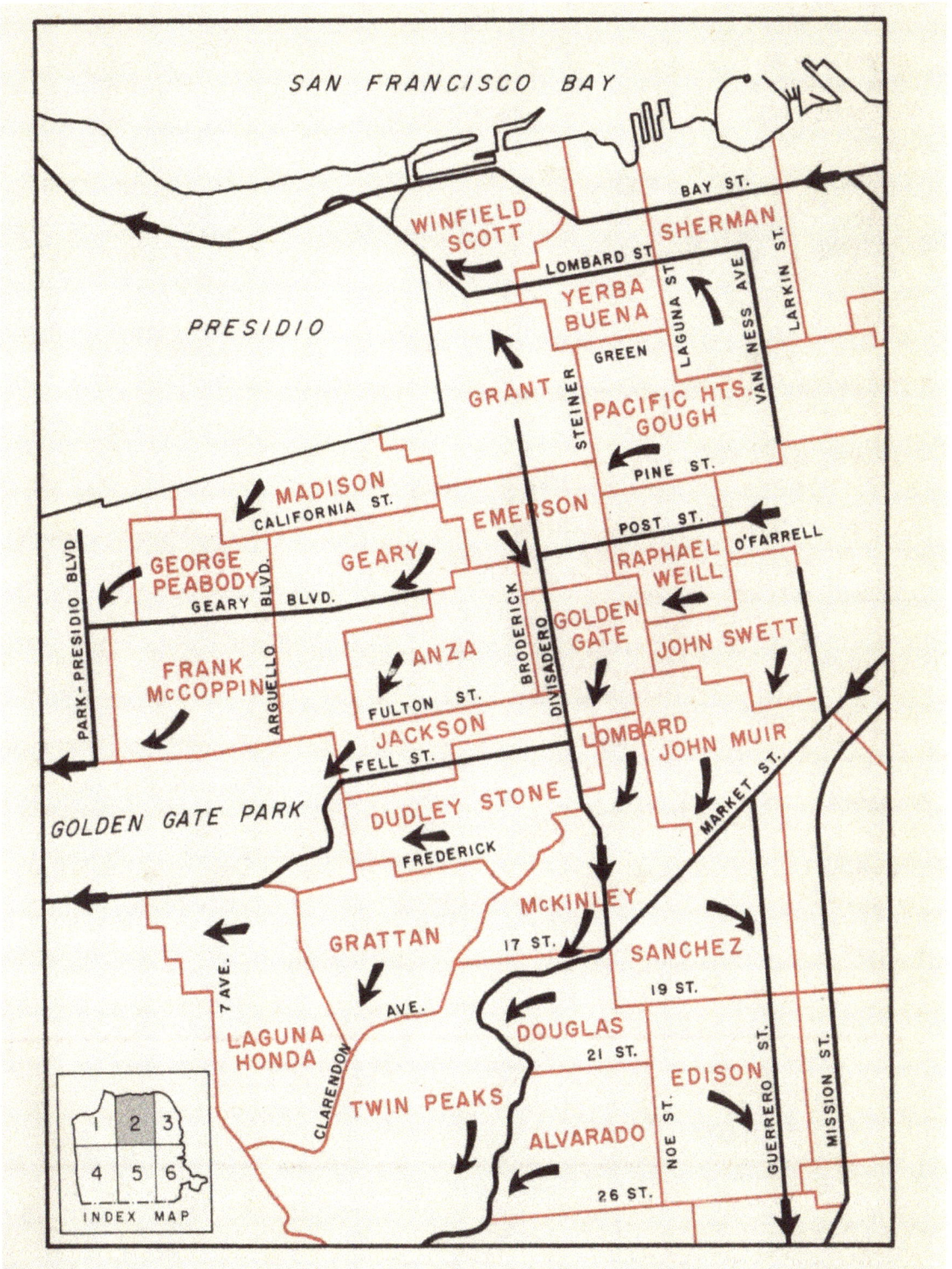

The civil defense agencies of Portland, Oregon; Vancouver, Washington; and Multnomah, Clackamas, Columbia, Hood River (Washington), Yamhill, and Clark (Washington) counties jointly published *Your Guide for Defense Against the H-Bomb*. The guide contained a Portland Evacuation Map (right) along with instructions on how to pre-

pare, what to do it an attack is imminent, and steps to take to survive radioactive fallout.

As with many civil defense publications in the 1950s, this one emphasized the fact that civilians are on the front line in the Atomic Age:

"PURPOSE . . .

The purpose of this guide is to tell you of the dangers to life and property in an H-Bomb attack and to tell you how you can best defend yourself against such an attack.

"CIVILIANS ON THE FRONT LINE . . .

As much as our nation strives for world peace, we must be prepared for a possible war. Without advance planning, there would be little hope if atomic attacks were made against principal American cities.

Oregon contains one of the critical target areas. Downtown Portland is considered as the aiming point for a target area which extends into several adjacent counties.

Civilians are now on the front line. In event of a major war, the first battlefield might be in this country, not abroad. The weapons could be nuclear as well as conventional bombs. Civilians would be among the first casualties, and a disaster of atomic magnitude would affect every phase of life.

Military defenses are being perfected, but there is no means to completely stop the penetration of all enemy bombers. One plane and one H-Bomb could destroy or severely damage most of the City of Portland.

"YOUR DECISION . . .

Although there are no easy solutions to atomic age civil defense, there are defenses against H-Bombs, the best being distance and shelter. Survival depends mainly on individual judgment and action.

"FOOD, WATER, CLOTHING

Following an enemy attack, thousands of persons would be in need of help. For your own protection, make sure your family is as self-sufficient as possible. Take food, water, clothing, bedding, radio, first aid kit, flashlight, and other essential items. Have members of your family help in assembling a "disaster kit." Keep the "kit" so it will be handy in your car or shelter.

"TRAFFIC CONTROL . . .

If you cannot immediately get into an Evacuation Route, move on parallel streets toward the outer edge of the city until you can get onto one. . . . Your help is needed to see that the free flow of traffic is not blocked at any time.

"ABOVE ALL . . .

Stay calm, be patient, obey instructions. With everyone's cooperation, all can move with less trouble and more speed."

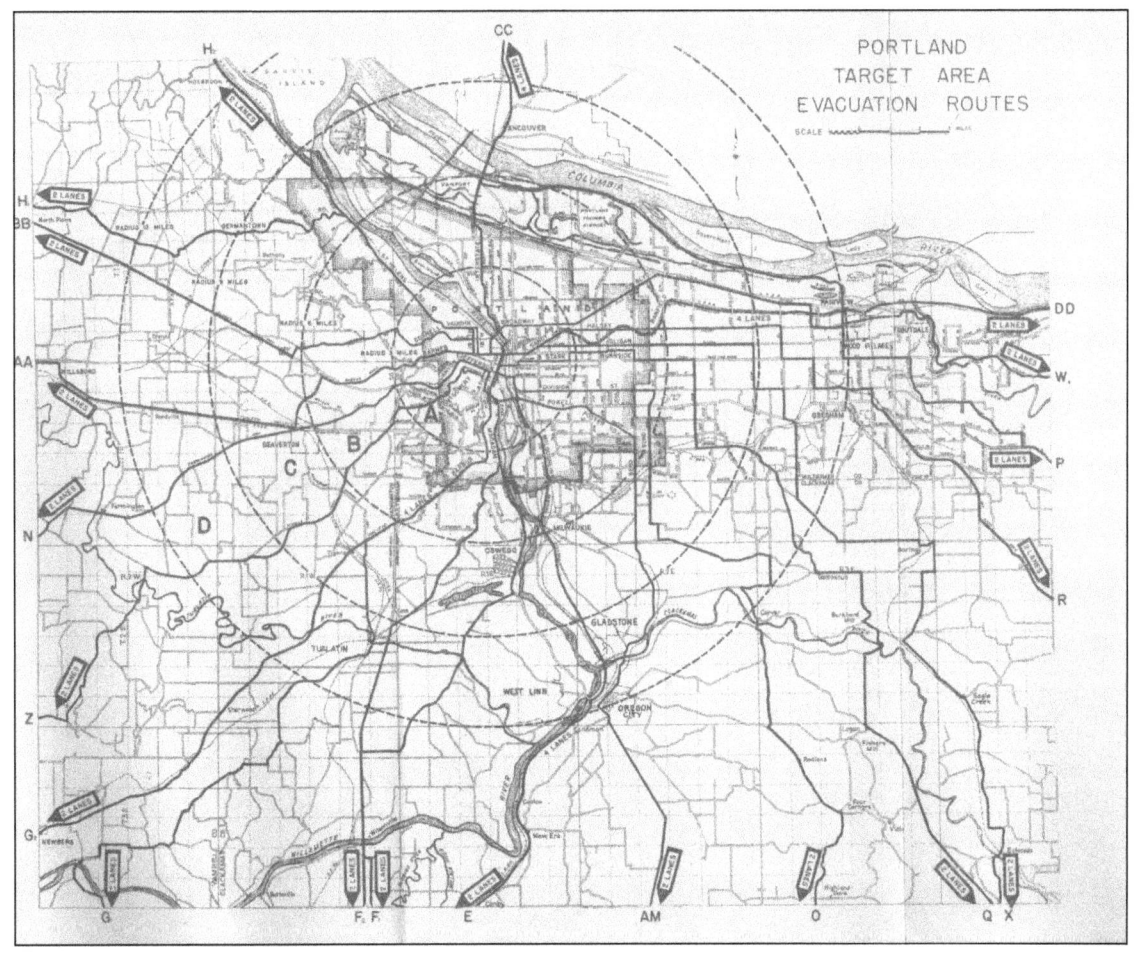

If there was no time to evacuate the city and you were forced to take shelter, the family's food supply became essential for survival. Most civil defense publications at least mentioned the importance of maintaining a supply of "safe" food and water; and civil de-

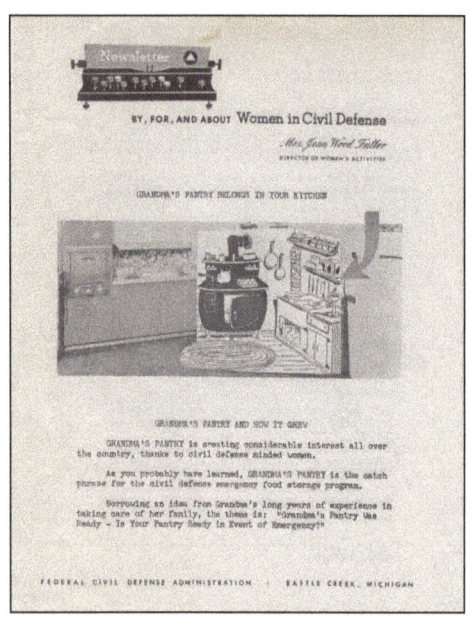

fense offices around the country held informative meetings on the subject. In New York, women in the New York State Civil Defense Commission went one step beyond by introducing a program called Grandma's Pantry, which referred to the past when every grandmother filled her pantry for a rainy day.

Grandma's Pantry soon spread from New York to Maine, where Inez Wing, civil defense director of women's activities for the Maine Civil Defense and Public Safety Agency, expanded the idea, issuing membership cards. The governor of Maine even declared Grandma's Pantry Week to bring attention to the program.

Grandma's Pantry became a nationwide civil defense program, endorsed by such organizations as Daughters of the American Revolution and Veterans of Foreign Wars Auxiliary.

The *By, For, and About Women in Civil Defense* newsletter, issued by the Federal Civil Defense Administration, read: "Today, as a result of the newly-created perils of possible enemy attack, GRANDMA'S PANTRY, or the re-creation of GRANDMA'S PANTRY in a sheltered area of the modern home, is once again a necessity.

"In case of disaster . . . your home might be isolated, or food shipments to your community might be disrupted.

GRANDMA'S PANTRY

WAS READY...

FEDERAL CIVIL DEFENSE ADMINISTRATION

"With a well-stocked pantry, you can be just as self-sufficient as Grandma was. Add a first-aid kit, flashlight, and a portable radio to this supply, and you will have taken the first important step in civil defense preparedness for your country.

"A minimum of seven days' supply of food and water or canned juices is recommended."

	Canned Meats—Canned Fish 24 oz. per person	Canned Vegetables 12-16 oz. per person	
Canned Fruit — 1 #1 can per person	Membership Card		Canned Milk 14 oz. per person
	GRANDMA'S PANTRY		
	A Civil Defense Project of the		
	Maine State Civil Defense and Public Safety Agency		
	HARRY A. MAPES, *Director*		
Canned Juices 64 oz. per person	This is to certify that I have qualified for "Grandma's Pantry Was Ready" Project		Canned Soups 12 oz. per person
	Signed:		
	Misc. Needs (See Grandma's Pantry Chart)	Beverages — Water 3-day supply per person	

Maine's Grandma's Pantry membership card.

WHAT SHOULD YOU PUT INTO A MODERN GRANDMA'S PANTRY?

The following items have been suggested for your GRANDMA'S PANTRY. Remember, a three-day supply is the minimum, a week's supply would be preferable.

Select your own requirements in quantities suitable to your personal or family needs. Check "pantry" at least once a month and rotate regularly. Remember bottled water is important, and it must be changed every six weeks. Items packed in glass or other than tin should be wrapped in paper for protection against breakage or damage. Keep in dry storage. Home canned supplies are good items too. All safety precautions should be taken for storage of cooking equipment using bottled gas or liquids.

CANNED MILK

Evaporated
Instant Non-fat Dry
Condensed

CANNED MEATS

Chicken
Fish
Meat Varieties
Stews
Bacon

CANNED SOUPS

All Varieties
Chowders

CANNED FRUIT

All Varieties

CANNED VEGETABLES

Potatoes
Peas
Baked Beans
String Beans
Corn
Tomatoes
Others

MISCELLANEOUS NEEDS

Flour - Also Prepared Types
Dry Yeast
Sugar
Salt and Pepper
Soap and Powder
Paper Supplies
Toilet Tissues
Safety Matches
Candles
Kitchen Silver, etc.
First Aid Kits
Olive Oil
Can Opener
Baby Foods
Pet Foods
Canned Heat
Shortening
Pails and Buckets
Crackers
Honey
Jam
Spreads
Dry Fruits
Cereals
Brown Bread

CANNED JUICES

Fruit and Vegetable

BEVERAGES

Coffee
Tea
Cocoa

Water, (Jugs)
Soft Drinks

In 1955, the Federal Civil Defense Administration published *Six Steps to Survival: If An Enemy Attacked Today Would You Know What to Do?* This small pamphlet reflected the FCDA's mission to make sure that every American knew what to do to survive an atomic attack:

"**Step One: Prepare your family for emergencies.** The family is the mainspring of civil defense. Get your family to work as a team in preparing for emergencies—whether from enemy attack or local disaster.

"**Step Two: Learn the civil defense public action signals.** Sirens, whistles, horns, or similar devices will warn you in case enemy attack is threatened. Memorize your local signals so you will know what to do instinctively."

"**Step Three: Know the Conelrad stations.** At the first indication of enemy bombers approaching the United States, all television and FM radio stations will go off the air. All standard (AM) stations will likewise go silent. The Conelrad stations, 640 or 1240, are your surest and fastest means of getting emergency civil defense information and instructions. Mark those numbers on your radio set—*now!*"

"**Step Four: Follow these evacuation principles.** The best protection against atomic or hydrogen bombs is—*don't be there!* In major cities, this means pre-attack evacuation.

"When you hear the alert signal, *do not use your telephone*. Instructions will be broadcast over your Conelrad frequency following the ALERT SIGNAL. You will be told what evacuation route to take. Take enough suitable clothing and emergency food supplies with you.

"Start now to make a family evacuation plan. Decide what food and clothing to bring. Decide where you will meet afterward if you get separated. Assign responsibilities."

"**Step Five: Build a home shelter.** In a sneak attack, or where there is insufficient warning for evacuation, any shelter is better than no shelter."

"**Step Six: Read these facts about radioactive fallout.** When atomic or hydrogen bombs are exploded close to the ground, they suck up into the mushroom cloud millions of tons of atomized earth and other materials. This material becomes highly radioactive.

"The best way to survive the hazards of radioactive fallout, or any other threat an enemy may use against us, is to be prepared—know the facts—learn what to do, *now!*

Grandma's Pantry was promoted in the 1956 FCDA pamphlet titled *Between You and Disaster*, which featured recommendations for a civil defense home storage plan. It read:

"Remember Grandma's Pantry, its shelves loaded with food, ready for any emergency, whether it be unexpected company or roads blocked for days by a winter's storm?

"Today, when we are vulnerable as always to the ravages of nature as well as the possibility of nuclear attack, every wise and thinking family will likewise prepare for emergencies with the modern equivalent of Grandma's Pantry.

"Whether you evacuate or take shelter in a Civil Defense emergency, one of the basic preparations recommended is an adequate food supply for your family. CD advises that you assemble a 7-day food supply in your home shelter area, and a 3-day evacuation-survival kit in your family automobile. This precaution might mean the difference between comfort and hardship—even between survival and starvation—in case of enemy attack or natural disaster.

"An H-bomb explosion can blanket an area many miles downwind with dangerous radioactive fallout. Following an enemy attack, essential services such as gas, electricity, and water, as well as normal channels of food distribution, would be disrupted. If this should happen, a family probably would have to depend wholly upon its own food and resources for survival. A Grandma's Pantry could be the family's only available supply of food."

The pamphlet recommended having at least a seven-day supply of food and water, with variables depending on the number of adults and children in the family.

"If the children are young," it emphasized, "the amounts can be decreased by one-fourth. If the children are infants, canned baby foods should be substituted for some of the other canned foods. Be sure to plan for old people or invalids."

Topeka, Kansas, became one of the nation's target cities because of its close proximity, only 160 miles, to Omaha, Nebraska, home of the Strategic Air Command; and Wichita, Kansas,, 140 miles away, where the B-47, capable of delivering atomic bombs, was built. For this reason, the Topeka-Shawnee County Civil Defense Office published the *Civil Defense Plan "A" and Map for Evacuation* in 1956. The pamphlet explained the large circles positioned on the map:

CIVIL DEFENSE
Plan "A" and Map For Evacuation
of City of Topeka and Its Environs

Provided by Your Topeka-Shawnee County Civil Defense Office
(Published November 1956, Revised November 1957)

FIRST READ AND STUDY THE ELEVEN BASIC QUESTIONS ON THE REVERSE SIDE, THEN THE TOPEKA MAP AND THE STATE MAP.

"The Kansas Map, which accompanies this plan, shows the QUALIFYING TARGETS FOR THE HYDROGEN BOMB, and the Danger areas are covered with circles. The Reception area boundaries, which evacuees will be cared for, are shone with distinguishing lines. Some of the area around the targets has not been designated as a Reception area because these areas may receive heavy fallout or may be the area for extensive Civil Defense operations for the benefit of the Target areas. THE FATE OF THIS GREAT NATION COULD DEPEND UPON THE ABILITY OF THE PEOPLE OF THE UNITED STATES TO ESCAPE AND RECOVER FROM THE EFFECT OF JUST ONE NATIONWIDE HYDROGEN BOMB STRIKE....

"If, over a period of time, a series of incidents and international tension should

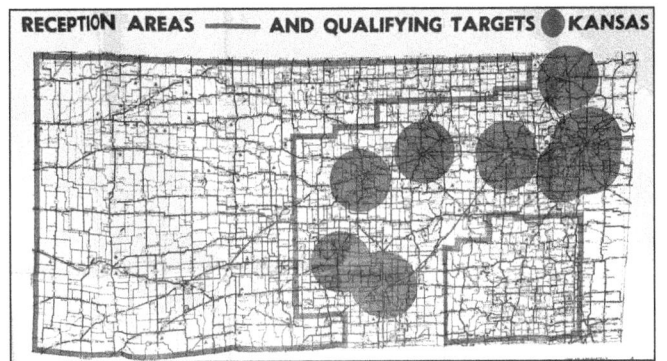

develop, indicating a threatened large scale attack on the U.S., it may be possible that schools, industries and other institutions and businesses may be closed or their operations limited, and some of the people evacuated considerably in advance of an actual air attack, adopting the most desirable procedures without hurry or confusion....

"In the near future, in order for the population to survive, many cities not target areas for bombing must plan for the evacuation of their cities for the sole purpose of avoiding fallout. Evacuation to avoid fallout will be from such areas, to such distances and to such places as announced by Conelrad, or by other means of communication and the evacuation routes will be used in such manner as the public is instructed.

The Ohio Valley Civil Defense Authority, serving the Cincinnati Metropolitan Area, issued its warning about an atomic attack in *Civil Defense: Will to Survive*, a 32-page booklet with several evacuation maps for those in the city (such as the one below showing escape routes to outlying counties). It also included illustrated instructions on the necessary actions to survive, with an emphasis on self-help:

"When any disaster comes, self-help is essential. Organized aid from Civil Defense authorities cannot possibly assist each individual immediately. . . .

"Your survival in disaster depends on you. Now is the time you and your family must inform yourselves. Make your decisions and determine individual action. This is the best way to insure survival."

The pamphlet included instructions on evacuation (opposite page) and the best way to reunite with one's family after evacuating the city (following pages).

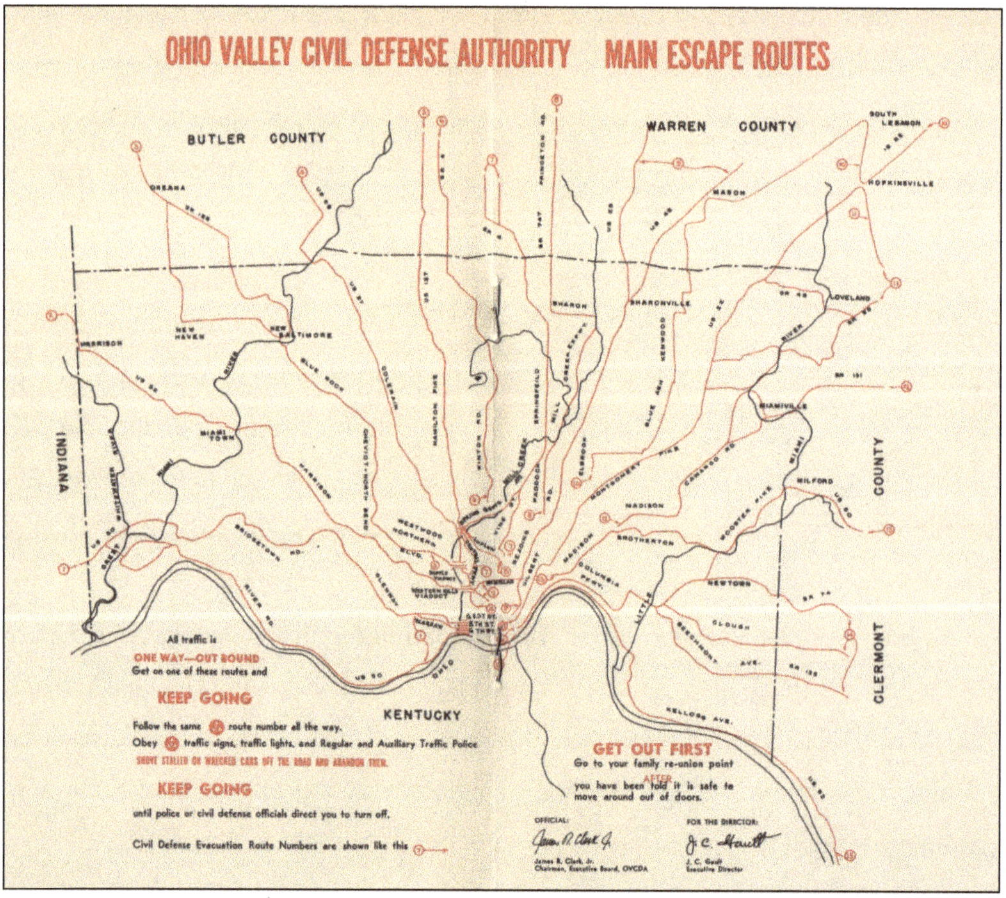

TO EVACUATE

When the warning comes and all people within the danger area are told to leave, get into or on some kind of vehicle—any kind of vehicle, including railroad trains, and move outward from downtown Cincinnati. If you are driving a vehicle, whether it is a passenger car, bus (except trolley) or truck, give rides to as many people as can crowd in or on it.

Streets and roads will soon be marked to show the routes to be followed. These routes have been carefully planned as a result of over two years' study. **FOLLOW THEM.** If you live in Northern Kentucky, for your own sake and your family's sake, do not try to cross the bridges. You will be returned by other routes to your destination in due course of time. If you do try to cross you would certainly be blocked by traffic at the southern end of the bridges, and you would only reduce your own chances, as well as the chances of many others.

If you are on foot and within a few blocks of a railroad yard, particularly the Union Terminal, or the yards along Millcreek, go to the yard and get on a train. **No ticket is necessary—Just get on,** no matter what kind of a train or car it is. The railroad company will run every locomotive and car they can move out of the danger area and there will be space for approximately 75,000 people. Once they are well out of the danger area, the train will be stopped near a reception center and you can then begin the reuniting process with any members of your family from whom you may have become separated.

DON'T TRY TO GO ANY PLACE IN PARTICULAR

JUST GET OUT

FOLLOW THE CD SIGNS AND TRAFFIC LIGHTS

AND THE LARGEST NUMBER OF PEOPLE

WILL ESCAPE

If you disregard the instructions, practically no one will escape.
Don't stop until you are far outside of the danger area—at least twenty miles from downtown Cincinnati—thirty miles is better.

When you do stop, get into the best cover you can find—get inside a building with windows and doors shut. A closed automobile is far better than nothing at all. Keep a radio tuned in at 640 or 1240 on the regular broadcast band.

DON'T TRY TO GO ANY PLACE IN PARTICULAR UNTIL YOU ARE TOLD THAT IT IS SAFE TO MOVE AROUND.

Eventually you will hear over the radio that it is safe to come out. Until such information is given to you,

Stay Under Cover

The Time Has Now Come to Reunite with Your Family

After the attack and after the radio has announced that it is safe to move around, go to the place which has been picked as a "Family Reunion Point" for all the people in your neighborhood. In this way you will be among people you know and who can help you find your family.

But that's not all. Civil Defense authorities are organizing all of these "Family Reunion Points," and when you get to yours, you will find that they are organized to give you food, shelter, and medical care, and, above all, by registration they will quickly bring you and your family together again.

. . . SO . . .

Look in the index in the back of this book to see what page the map of your neighborhood is on.

Your Family Reunion Point is the One Listed in the Reunion Index

On the Reunion index pages you will find the name of the city or village which is the reunion point for the neighborhoods shown on the maps.

AFTER the attack, and AFTER you are told it is SAFE TO COME OUT OF SHELTER AND MOVE AROUND, go in the best way you can to your proper Family Reunion point.

Copies of a special book are being placed in the hands of the police and Civil Defense authorities of every city and village in southwestern Ohio and southeastern Indiana, so that if when the time comes you don't know where your proper re-union point is, you can find out from them.

When You Get to Your Reunion Point

Ask for and go to the Registration Center. The Civil Defense workers there will take your name and address. They will then check their records to see if any other members of your family have registered. If they have, you will be sent to them at once. If they have not, you will be given lodging and other necessary care, and the other members of your family will be sent to you as soon as they come in to register.

Some Good Advice

In case of attack, as in any disaster, the best help you can get is the help you give yourself. And you cannot help yourself or anyone else if you are dead.

Your first duty is to save your own and as many other lives as you can. If you are away from home or otherwise separated from your family,

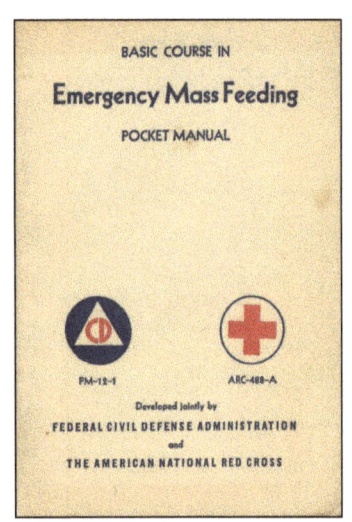

One of the most challenging aspects of a major disaster—and especially one following an enemy attack—is aiding the survivors. In respect to the aftermath of an atomic attack, housing would be important, but more critical would be the feeding of perhaps hundreds of thousands of survivors in the nation's major cities.

To addresses this problem, the Federal Civil Defense Administration and The American National Red Cross introduced a mass feeding program, with the FCDA publishing the *Basic Course in Emergency Mass Feeding Pocket Manual* in 1957. The manual provided instructions on setting up and managing a program to feed those fortunate to have survived. It covered water, waste disposal, dishwashing, duties of food workers, precautions with radioactive contamination, and constructing emergency stations, such as the dishwashing and hand-washing facilities shown below.

FCDA Administrator Val Peterson and Alfred Gruenther, president of The American National Red Cross, penned the introduction, which read, "This Pocket Manual is a guide for uniform training of personnel of both agencies in emergency mass-feeding operations.

"This uniform training is designed to provide our communities with a reservoir of trained citizens with the knowledge and skills to conduct large feeding operations in time of national emergencies created either by natural disaster or enemy attack.

"In case of a major emergency, these trained food workers may be called upon as needed to work either through the Red Cross or Civil Defense. In a natural disaster, food workers will be under the direction of the Red Cross; in an enemy-caused disaster, under the direction of Civil Defense.

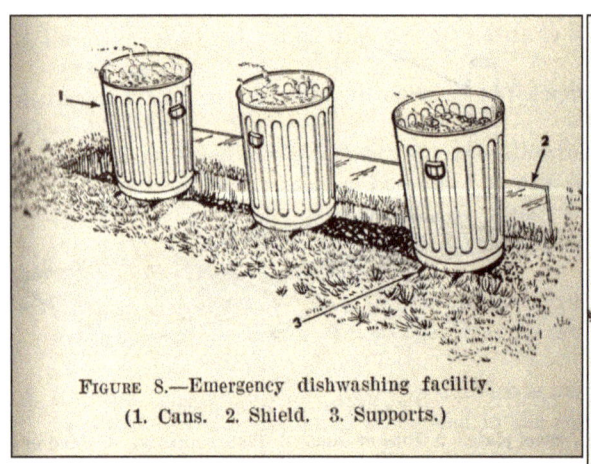

FIGURE 8.—Emergency dishwashing facility.
(1. Cans. 2. Shield. 3. Supports.)

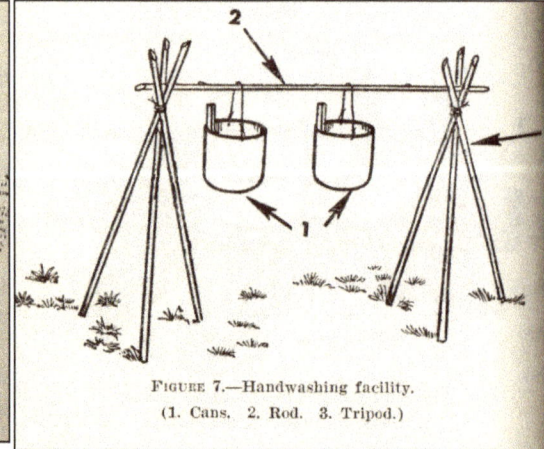

FIGURE 7.—Handwashing facility.
(1. Cans. 2. Rod. 3. Tripod.)

Civil defense agencies were not the only entities issuing publications about the threat of atomic warfare. Private companies, from liquor stores to insurance agencies to automobile dealers, also published and/or distributed civil defense booklets.

In St. Louis, the G. F. Kiesel Company, which specialized in fuel oil, space heaters, and stokers, published *The Atomic Bomb and You: What to Do In Case of Atomic Attack*. The 44-page booklet covered all aspects of the atomic bomb's impact and the steps for survival, and used illustrations to enhance the instructions.

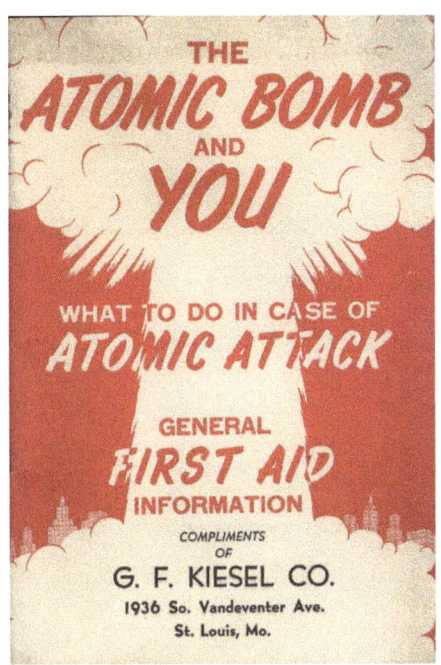

A good scrubbing after blast will remove radioactive particles clinging to skin.

Remove injured from scene of fire only to save a life. Otherwise wait for doctor.

Handkerchief over face will keep you from inhaling radioactive mist from water burst.

Nail drapes over broken windows. This will help keep out radioactive dust or fog.

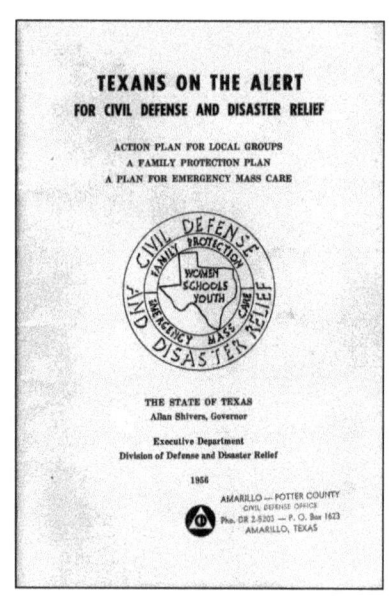

The Texas Division of Defense and Disaster Relief published a 64-page handbook in 1956 titled *Texans on the Alert for Civil Defense and Disaster Relief*. The handbook focused primarily on women, schools, and youth "with the hope that . . . it will inspire and encourage the continuing efforts of all Texans to minimize and alleviate the effects of any disaster with which we might be confronted."

The handbook was divided into three sections: Action Plans for Local Groups; A Family Protection Plan; and A Plan for Emergency Mass Care, which included information on mass shelter, mass feeding, and mass clothing.

The role of women in civil defense was heavily emphasized, pointing out that 60 percent of the 17 million volunteers needed by the FCDA must be "hard-working, well-trained" women. It went on to describe the various ways women could become involved, including the Warden Service; home nursing; the Ground Observer Corps; the Messenger Service; and Health and Emergency Medical Services.

Youth were also encouraged to become involved by volunteering at their local community civil defense office; distributing civil defense materials to the school and the community; taking first-aid and home-care classes; and volunteering for the Ground Observer Corps. School administrators were encouraged to develop plans for self-protection, including designating wardens; conducting regular drills; starting communication systems; and ensuring that schools were well prepared for a disaster situation.

ACTION PLANS FOR LOCAL GROUPS

You and Civil Defense, published by the New York State Civil Defense Commission, provided a comprehensive overview of the various warning signals, shelters, the utilization of warning time (below), and post-bomb rescue and recovery.

It warned that if an atomic attack occurred, the nation's military forces would respond swiftly, but the mission of civil defense would remain the rescue and relief of those who survived the attack.

The booklet made a harsh observation: "Should such an eventuality occur, our civilian population would then be plunged into the special horrors that warfare in the nuclear age could bring."

UTILIZATION OF WARNING TIME

STATE AND LOCAL PLANS take into account the use of possible available warning time.

1 If an attack occurs without warning the following action should be taken — *"Duck and Cover."* Duck and Cover means just that. It is the action you take between the light or flash of the explosion and the arrival of the blast wave. The bomb's flash travels at the speed of light, and the blast wave travels at the speed of sound.

2 If warning time is 30 minutes or less, the recommended action is — *"Take Cover."* Unless there is sufficient time available to execute a "Go Home" or an evacuation, Take Cover is the only action left to execute.

3 If more time is available, Civil Defense authorities will issue a *"Go Home"* order. You would then proceed to your home where members of your family would assemble and prepare for possible evacuation if ordered. In the available time your basement fallout shelter should be made ready for possible occupancy. A survival kit of essential items should be prepared with blankets, water, food and medical supplies to take with you should you be required to evacuate. You must take measures to safeguard your valuables.

Detailed plans exist for the reception and care of evacuees in the support areas surrounding every target zone.

Another concern if an enemy attack should occur was responding to the needs of pregnant women about to give birth. In 1956, the Bureau of Maternal and Child Health of the New York State Department of Health, in cooperation with the department's Office of

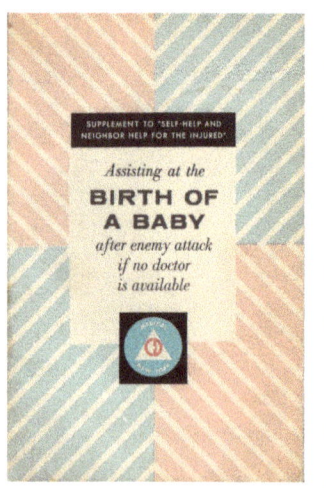

Medical Defenses, published a special civil-defense supplement to *Self-Help and Neighbor Help to the Injured*. The supplement was titled *Assisting at the Birth of a Baby After Enemy Attack If No Doctor Is Available*.

The 28-page booklet covered each phase of child birth: labor pains, actual birthing process, and care of the mother and baby after the birth.

The opening page, titled "Bombs and Babies," warned that an atomic attack can cause the birth of a baby ahead of the expected time:

"This occurs because of the fear and exertion of the expectant mother. During the first 48 hours after an attack, medical or nursing care may not be available for deliveries (births) of babies—since all personnel will be working in medical installations caring for critically injured survivors. Hence, as many persons as possible should learn how to give care of the mother and baby.

"Almost all births occur without trouble. But there are many things a neighbor or member of the family can learn to do to help the mother and baby during delivery. In addition to learning how to care for normal deliveries, it is also necessary that persons learn how to recognize abnormal signs or symptoms which demand that the mother be seen by a doctor and hospitalized if necessary."

The publication included detailed, step-by-step instructions on helping during labor and during delivery, as well as instructions on caring for the newborn baby.

Counties throughout the state of New York also conducted training and drills for civil defense personnel to help them prepare for a birth without the presence of a doctor. When completed, the New York Office of Civil Defense issued a certificate of completion.

4 WHEELS TO SURVIVAL

Always Be Sure...

Your car is mechanically sound

Your car radio works

Your gas tank is more than half full

Your battery is alive

Your tires are safe

YOUR FAMILY CAR — *The difference between Life and Death?*

You may think your family car is indispensable under ordinary conditions -- but how much more important it becomes in an emergency. Here are some of the bonuses a well-cared-for automobile can give you:

SHELTER

Automobiles provide a degree of protection against blast, as well as radioactive fallout. Remember, though--LOWER your windows before an attack to equalize pressures and prevent glass breakage, and RAISE your windows after an attack to keep out dust and debris (which may be radioactive).

FOOD

"Grandma's Pantry" was never like this--but your 7-day food supply should be kept in a carton, ready to put in the trunk of your family car. Everything to make your family self-sufficient for several days, if necessary, should be included. Your car can be a portable house.

INFORMATION

If your car radio dial is not already marked, mark the 640 and 1240 Conelrad frequencies, for they will be your source of information and instruction under attack conditions.

MOBILITY

Pre-attack evacuation, as well as many other civil defense activities, depends upon your ability to move away from approaching danger. Learn how to conserve gasoline--you may not be able to buy any. And keep on hand good maps of your city and the surrounding area.

LAST BUT NOT LEAST... *the rules of safe driving and courtesy to others become doubly important in an emergency.* REMEMBER

DO
- Obey police and civil defense authorities
- If you have room, pick up pedestrians
- If your car stalls, get it off the road

DON'T
- Crowd or try to beat the other fellow
- Be impatient or lean on the horn— you may panic others.

The automobile served as the means of surviving an atomic attack by evacuating the city.

The Bell Telephone Company of Pennsylvania, in cooperation with the Pennsylvania State Council of Civil Defense and the Eastern Air Defense Forces, published *The Big Call* to explain the procedures of the Ground Observer Corps, the nation's air-raid warning

THE BIG CALL

system manned by thousands of volunteers nationwide.

As illustrated below, GOC volunteers scanned the skies for approaching enemy bombers and, if spotted, report the location to a Filter Center—called an "Aircraft Flash." At its height, the GOC had some 800,000 volunteers watching the skies throughout the nation.

"At the Filter Center," the booklet read, "civilian volunteers under the direction of Air Force men, plot plane information on a large table known as a 'Filter Board.' After two reports on a plane, the Filter Center can tell the direction in which the plane is headed.

"It then puts in a call, on a private telephone line, to an Air Defense Direction Center. This Center may have already detected the approach of the suspect plane by its radar. The Air Force men here evaluate the reports and check on whether the plane is friendly.

"If the approaching plane or planes cannot be identified as friendly, the Air Defense Detection Center summons interceptor planes into the air from a nearby airfield, using a private telephone wire. Anti-aircraft batteries are alerted over a wide area. It also notifies the Air Defense Control Center, which commands a large

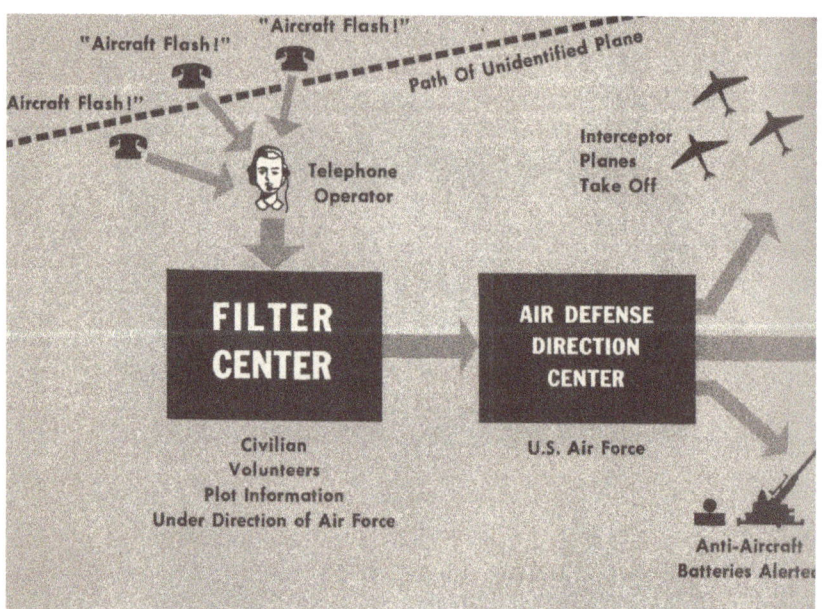

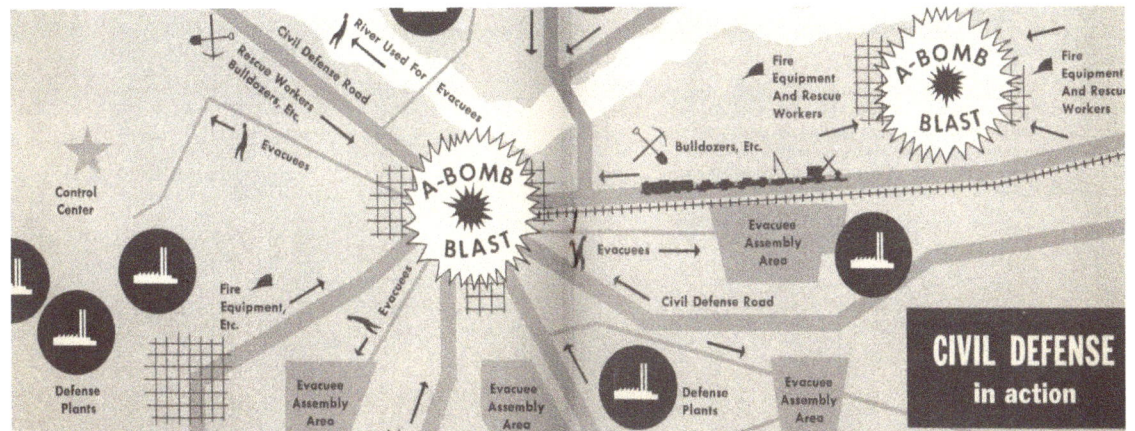

Illustration shows the impact of an atomic bomb on a typical city, with evacuation routes indicated.

section of the United States.

"This Control Center then notifies other branches of the Armed Services—Army, Navy, Air Force, as well as the Civil Aeronautics Authority and the Royal Canadian Air Force. It decides whether the civilian population should be alerted. If it so decides, it orders a Yellow (preliminary) Alert by means of an extensive private telephone network. . . .

"If the Air Defense Control Center decides that an actual attack is impending and that a public warning is necessary, the officer on duty at the key-point hears the announcement and dials 'R' for the Red Alert signal. The area under its jurisdiction is alerted at once by air raid sirens. Local radio stations also broadcast the Red Alert.

"If the attack is repelled or diverted, the Center decides that the emergency is ended and the 'White' or 'All Clear' signal is passed along in the same manner. This signal is a long, steady blast on the siren.

"That, briefly, is how the air raid warning system is set up. . . .

"We urge you to got a step further and identify yourself with Civil Defense as a volunteer worker in times of disaster."

Civil Defense Agencies In Local Communities

Key Point Warning Stations

"THE BIG CALL"

AIR DEFENSE CONTROL CENTER FOR LARGE AREA OF U.S.

U.S. ARMY · U.S. AIR FORCE · U.S. NAVY CIVIL AERONAUTICS AUTHORITY ROYAL CANADIAN AIR FORCE

Civil defense publications in the 1950s focused primarily on family survival, but the federal government also provided advice to state education departments on the importance of ensuring the survival of the younger generation—the generation that might be needed to rebuild the nation after an atomic attack.

The definitive publication on this topic was issued by the Civil Defense Education Project in the Office of Education, a department in the U.S. Department of Health, Education, and Welfare. Titled *Education for National Survival: A Handbook on Civil Defense for Schools*, the publication provided an overview of the national civil defense structure from the federal level to states and local agencies. Most important, it included extensive instructions on the responsibilities of educators to prepare students for the Atomic Age. Educators included state departments of education, school boards, principals, teachers, and non-teaching personnel (e.g., school nurses and bus drivers).

Among the steps recommended were equipping schools with shelters; conducting evacuation exercises; establishing control centers and communication systems for emergencies; and practicing post-attack recovery procedures.

Beginning in the late 1940s, elementary and secondary schools began to modify their curricula to incorporate information about the atomic bomb and atomic energy into regular classroom subjects, such as English, science, mathematics, speech, history, and art. The new approach, called "atomics," expanded in the 1950s as the need to make students aware of a possible atomic attack and ensure their survival became another dimension of the nation's civil defense plan.

Education for National Survival, building on the Operation Atomic Vision's recommendations in 1948, provided guidelines for civil defense instructions in elementary and secondary schools, with an emphasis on the "atomics" approach.

"Civil defense education," it read, "should be part of the experiences of every school -age person. It prepares the student to survive physical disaster and enables him, as a future citizen, to protect himself and others, serve his community, and help strengthen the Nation in time of emergency.

"Instruction in civil defense cannot be a packaged program. It is not something to be taught for a few days or weeks and then laid aside. Rather, it must be appropriately included at many points in the total curriculum where its application and utilization are compatible with ongoing classroom activities.

"Many areas of the curriculum can be modified to include civil defense education. Science classes provide opportunities to teach understandings of the technology of modern warfare and natural disasters. Other teaching opportunities are to be found in the broad fields of the social studies, health, safety, and physical education. The importance of extra-class activities and their usefulness in civil defense education should not be overlooked."

State education departments did, in fact, adopt "atomics" at all levels: from kindergarten to senior high school. Civil defense planning guides for teachers contained detailed steps on how to teach students not only about the atomic bomb and atomic energy, but about such topics as international relations and the importance of good citizenship.

FALLOUT WARNINGS, 1958-1963

The year 1957 saw two significant events that escalated concerns about a nuclear war. In July 1957, the United States' test of the Atlas, an ICBM with a range of 5,000 miles, was a total disaster, with the missile rising some 5,000 feet in the air then crashing back to earth. A month later, on August 26, the Soviet Union successfully tested an intercontinental ballistic missile (ICBM) capable, according to the Soviet Union, of reaching "any part of the world." Now, rather than taking hours for Soviet bombers to reach the United States with nuclear bombs, it would only take minutes with ICBM's capability of reaching speeds up to 20,000 miles per hour.

Then, on October 4, 1957, a Soviet R-7 ICBM launched Sputnik, the first artificial satellite, into space. Sputnik caught the nation by surprise and raised concerns about the potential of the R-7 ICBM delivering a nuclear bomb into United States air space.

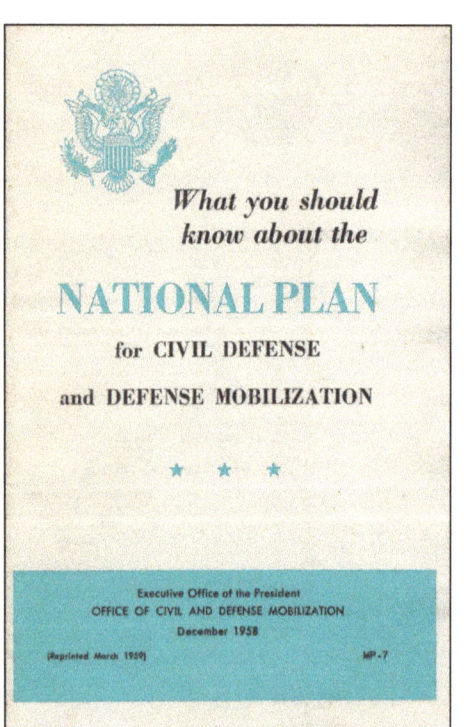

Although the U.S. successfully launched its first satellite, Explorer, on January 31, 1958, it came after the Soviet Union's successful launch of Sputnik 2 with the first living creature, a dog, sent into space.

The government responded to the potential new threat in 1958 by establishing a national plan and publishing a booklet describing the plan titled *What You Should Know About the National Plan for Civil Defense and Defense Mobilization*. The booklet focused on reassuring the American people that the government would provide leadership, direction, coordination, and guidance "necessary for an effective civil defense and defense mobilization in this Nation."

In other words, the plan guaranteed support for civil defense, but it emphasized the need for every family to be proactive in learning about and implementing civil defense measures that would help ensure their survival.

"Preparation to survive an H-bomb is more sensible than guessing whether or not it will ever be used against us," it read.

"Today, and for some years hence, it is assumed that enemy weapons will be predominantly nuclear. The use of biological and chemical agents is also possible. Today, the weapons can be delivered by manned airplanes. Within the next few years, the delivery could be predominantly by missile. Today, the warning time between detection and arrival of incoming enemy planes is zero to three hours. Within a few years, the missile could reduce the warning time to half an hour, or even to zero. Strategic warning in advance of an attack is a possibility.

"If the nuclear burst is at or near the surface of the earth, the secondary and widespread threat will be radioactive fallout. . . . However, not everybody will to too close to the burst and not everybody will be exposed thereafter to fallout radiation so intense that it cannot be cut to safety by shielding. Studies of possible attack patterns and their probable effects indicate that a large majority of the total population can survive.

"The operations outlined in the National Plan will help assure that this majority will be as large as possible and will help to bring about national survival, recovery, and victory."

In an effort to reassure Americans that the civil defense program was continuing to expand, the pamphlet pointed out that 47 states, two territories, and 230 metropolitan areas had prepared survival plans in case of an attack by Soviet bombers delivering hydrogen bombs (before the introduction of ICBMs).

The NATIONAL PLAN and YOU

The primary purpose of the National Plan is to provide protection for YOU, your family, your neighbors, and your fellow-Americans. But the Plan will work only if YOU — 175 million of YOU — make it work. The National Government can provide the blueprint, set up the production lines, and achieve a partnership among Federal, State, and local governments. But the real strength of the program can be achieved only with the active support and participation of all citizens.

On July 1, 1958, President Dwight Eisenhower's administration created the Office of Civil and Defense Mobilization (OCDM), which consolidated the functions of the Office of Defense Mobilization and the Federal Civil Defense Administration. In 1961, under the administration of President John Kennedy, the OCDM's civil defense functions were transferred to the Office of Civil Defense in the Defense Department, with the remaining functions reorganized as the Office of Emergency Planning.

The OCDM continued the many responsibilities of the FCDA, including publishing civil defense pamphlets, such as *Emergency Sanitation at Home*, *Individual and Family Survival Requirements*, and *Home Protection Exercises*.

Even those lucky enough to survive the blast from a nuclear bomb would most likely be without any services or ability to acquire food, medical supplies, and, more important, drinking water. In the aftermath of an attack, city pipes could possibly have leaking sewage, poisonous chemicals, radioactive materials, or disease-carrying organisms from biological warfare.

"You and your family could get along for quite awhile without food, if necessary," read *Emergency Sanitation at Home*, "but you must have safe water to drink."

BEFORE DISASTER STRIKES

YOU SHOULD HAVE....

YOU SHOULD KNOW....

Where to find safe water	How to dispose of garbage
How to turn off water service valve	How to dispose of human wastes
How to purify water	How to make soil bags
What foods to store and how to prepare them	What to do with frozen foods
What foods are unsafe	

Stored water or other liquid (7 gals. per person)	A covered pail for bathroom purposes
A 2-week supply of proper foods, paper plates and napkins	Toilet tissue, paper towels, sanitary napkins, disposable diapers, soap
Cooking and eating utensils, measuring cup, can and bottle openers, pocket knife and matches	Rubber sheeting and special equipment for the sick
Special foods for babies and the sick	Grocery bags, week's supply of newspapers for sanitary uses, waterproof gloves
Large garbage can to keep garbage	2 pts. of household chlorine, 1 qt. of 5 percent DDT
Smaller can for human wastes	Wrench, screwdriver, shovel, and other tools

"To insure a safe supply for emergency use, store enough drinking water for your family right now. You should have available at least seven gallons of water or other fluids for each member of your family."

Individual and Family Survival Requirements also stressed the importance of a shelter reserve food supply—foods that could keep for months without refrigeration and require little or no cooking.

"Foods canned in metal and glass will stay in good condition for 6 or more months," it read, "if kept in a dry place, protected from sun and dust, and kept at a fairly cool temperature—preferably not above 70 degrees F. or below freezing. To keep food in paper boxes as long as months, place them in tightly closed metal cans or cabinets and store them under the dry, cool, clear conditions specified for canned foods, so that rodents and insects are not likely to attack them.

"It is good practice to rotate foods in cans at least once or twice a year and foods in paper boxes at least every 3 months. This will ensure having a reserve supply of food that is good-tasting.

"As food on the reserve shelf is used for meals for unexpected company and the family, replace it, putting the older stocks in front of the new supply."

(ANNEX 2-INDIVIDUAL ACTION)

Individual
and Family
Survival
Requirements

MP-2-1
NATIONAL PLAN APPENDIX SERIES

Executive Office of the President
OFFICE OF CIVIL AND DEFENSE MOBILIZATION

TABLE 1—*Guide for shelter reserve food supply*

Kind of food	Need per person		Remarks
	Daily	*2 weeks*	
1. Milk	Equivalent of 2 glasses (fluid)	Equivalent of 7 qts. (fluid)	Each of the following is about the equivalent of one quart of fluid milk: Three 6-oz. cans of evaporated milk. One 14½ oz. can of evaporated milk. Three to 3½ ozs. of nonfat dry milk.
2. Canned meat, poultry, fish, dry beans, and peas	2 servings	28 servings (about 8 to 9 lbs.)	Amounts required for one serving of each food are as follows: Canned meat, poultry, fish—2 to 3 ozs. Canned mixtures of meat, poultry, or fish with vegetables, rice, macaroni, spaghetti, noodles, or dry beans—8 ozs. Thick soups containing meat, poultry, fish, or dry beans or peas—one-half of a 10½-oz. can (condensed).
3. Fruits and vegetables	3 to 4 servings	42 to 56 servings (about 21 lbs. canned)	Amounts required for one serving of each food are as follows: Canned juices—4 to 6 ozs., single strength. Canned fruit and vegetables—4 ozs. Dried fruit—1½ ozs.
4. Cereals and baked goods	3 to 4 servings	42 to 56 servings (about 5 to 7 lbs.)	Amounts required for one serving of each food are as follows (selection depends on extent of cooking possible): Cereal: Ready-to-eat, puffed—¼ oz. Ready-to-eat, flaked—¾ oz. Other ready-to-eat and uncooked—1 oz. Crackers, cookies—1 oz. Canned bread, steamed puddings, and cake—1 to 2 ozs. Flour, flour mixes—1 oz. Macaroni, spaghetti, noodles: Dry—¾ oz. Cooked, canned—6 ozs.
5. Spreads for bread and crackers	According to family practices		Examples: Cheese spreads. Peanut and other nut butters. Jam, jelly, marmalade, preserves. Sirup, honey. Apple and other fruit butters. Relish, catsup, mustard.
6. Hydrogenated fats and vegetable oils		Up to 1 lb. or 1 pt.	Amount needed depends upon extent of cooking possible.

81

A FAMILY ACTION PROGRAM

HOME PROTECTION *exercises*

MP-1
(Misc. Publication)

EXECUTIVE OFFICE OF THE PRESIDENT
Office of Civil and Defense Mobilization

(Slightly revised July 1960 ... Reprinted March 1961)

Home Protection Exercises, a 32-page booklet, began by warning that if you are caught unprepared for an emergency, such as an atomic attack, "what you don't know about protecting your home and family could be costly—even fatal." To ensure that this did not occur, the booklet provided extensive information on what it called the eight most important family action exercises:

1. What to do when the warning signals sound.

2. Preparation of your shelter.

3. Home fire protection.

4. Home fire fighting.

5. Emergency action to save lives.

6. What to do if someone is trapped.

7. Provision of safe food and water in emergencies.

8. Home nursing.

"Study these exercises," it read. "Explain them to your family. Then rehearse them. Make a game of them, if you like, but keep in mind that the purpose is the serious one of learning to

EXERCISE 2

PREPARATION OF YOUR SHELTER

meet and cope with any disaster or emergency that may affect your home and family."

Preparing a home shelter was the second most important exercises. The booklet acknowledged that with the power of the hydrogen bomb, evacuation was the best way to ensure survival; if there was not enough warning time, however, the booklet stressed that the only hope for survival was a shelter, even though "the construction of family shelters against and blast and heat effects of large nuclear weapons would be impracticable because of building and cost factors."

The alternative, if one is far enough away from the initial blast, was a fallout shelter to protect against radioactive fallout. "A family shelter against radioactive fallout has an added advantage for those who live in the "tornado belt" of the country, because it can serve equally well as refuge and protection from the devastation caused by these violent storms.

The third most important exercise was home fire protection, as shown in the illustration below.

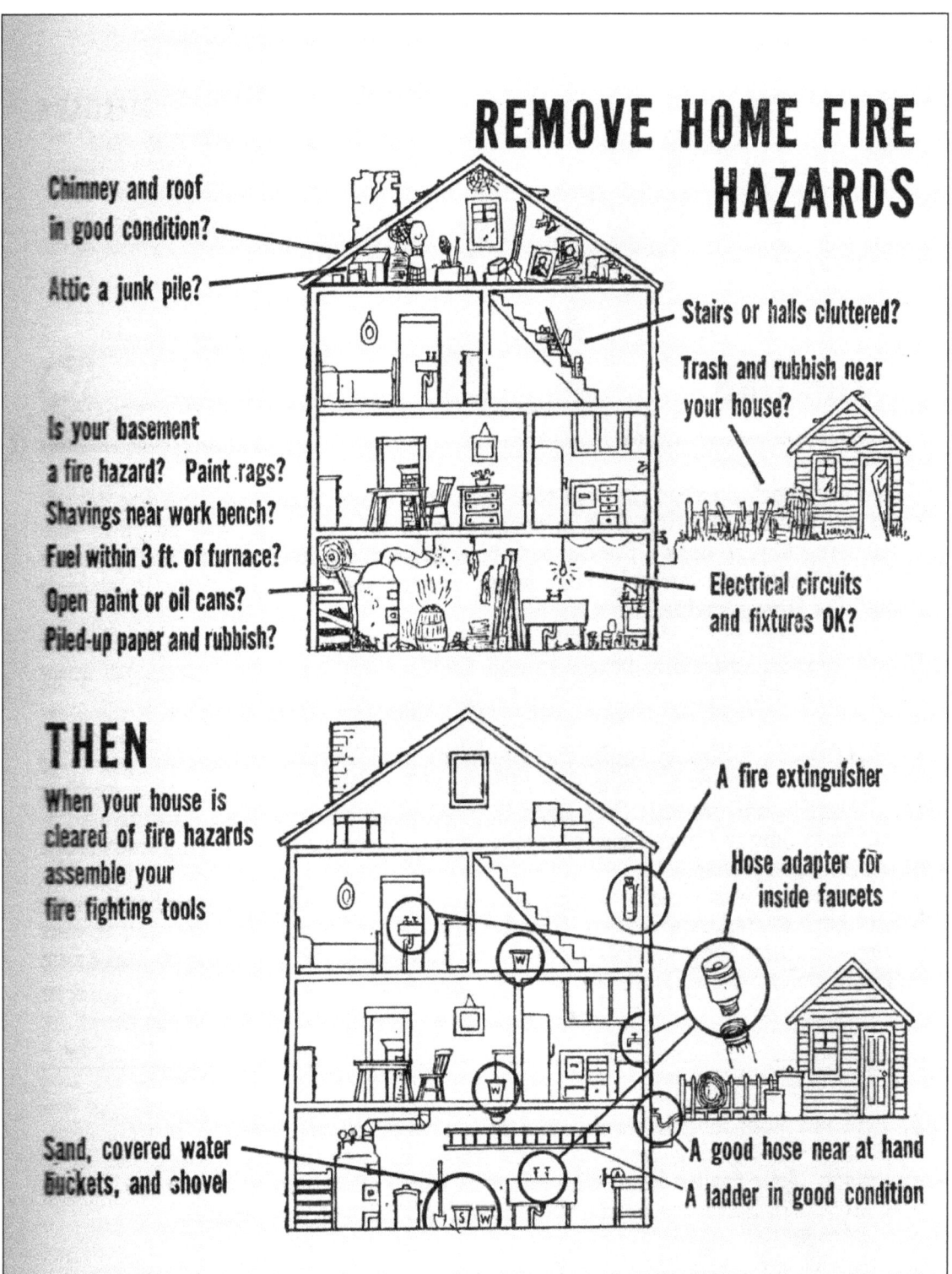

The Family Fallout Shelter, a 32-page booklet, provided instructions for building or installing various types of shelters, depending on one's personal situation: the basement concrete block shelter (below), the pre-shaped metal shelter (opposite page top), the underground concrete shelter (opposite page bottom), and shelters in apartment buildings.

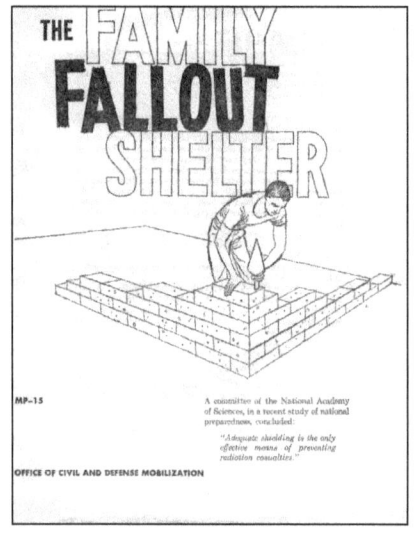

"We do not want war," it read. "We do not know whether there will be a war. But we know that forces hostile to us possess weapons that could destroy us if we were unready. These weapons create a new threat—radioactive fallout that can spread death anywhere.

"This is why we must prepare.

"No matter where you live, a fallout shelter is necessary insurance. It will not be needed except in emergency. But in emergency it will be priceless—as priceless as your life."

Pre-shaped metal shelter.

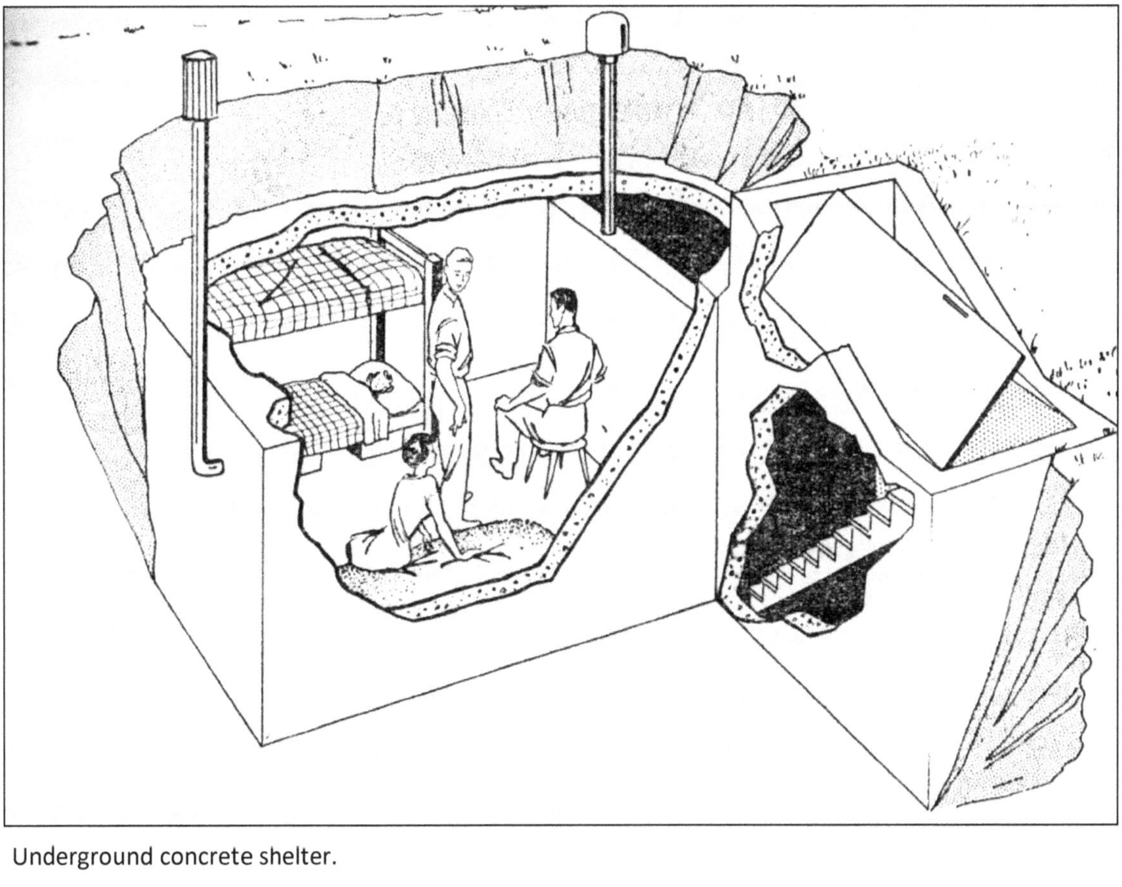

Underground concrete shelter.

In 1958, the U.S. Department of Agriculture, in an effort to keep pace with the development of hydrogen bombs, published a revised edition of *Radioactive Fallout on the Farm*, which covered such topics as fallout's impact on livestock, land, and crops. The bulletin was structured in a question-and-answer format with recommendations based on the expertise of scientists, engineers, public health officials, civil defense authorities, among others. The purpose was to ensure that America's farmers and ranchers understood the deadly effects of fallout.

"An enemy attack with a nuclear weapon," it read, "could cause radioactive contamination many miles downwind from the target area. Radioactive particles produced by the bomb give off destructive rays, which in certain situations can injure—and kill—human beings and animals, and can make farm lands and crops dangerous to use. These particles are called radioactive fallout."

For livestock, the bulletin advised putting them in barns or other farm buildings if there was adequate advance warning of an atomic attack.

"A reasonably well-built shelter prevents fallout from settling on the animals' bodies and may reduce the intensity of external radiation. It also protects against the animals eating contaminated food."

The bulletin identified three primary consequences of heavy fallout on crops and pasture land:

1. Farm workers may not be able to manage and cultivate land safely for some time because of radiation hazard.

2. It may not be advisable to permit animals to graze because of the danger of internal and external radiation.

3 Radioactive materials that are deposited on the edible portions of plants or absorbed through the roots are a potential long-term hazard to human beings and animals."

The U.S. Department of Agriculture published another bulletin in 1961 on food. *Family Food Stockpile for Survival*, or *Home and Garden Bulletin No. 77*, contained sample meal plans (below); how to store and replace food; equipment needed for cooking and serving; and advice on storing a safe water supply. Whereas a seven-day stockpile of food and water was adequate in the early 1950s, families now needed at least a 14-day supply of "survival foods" with the dramatic increase in the effects of the more   powerful hydrogen bomb.

"Survival foods may vary from a single cracker-type food, such as rye or wheat wafers or specially prepared biscuits, to a fairly complete assortment of familiar foods.

"Stockpile foods should be in cans, jars, or sealed paper or plastic containers. Select foods that will last for months without refrigeration and can be eaten with little or no cooking.

"Take into consideration the needs and preferences of family members, storage space, and ability to rotate the stored foods in family meals. Familiar foods are likely to be more acceptable in times of stress.

"If necessary, include special kinds of milk and strained, chopped, or other specially prepared foods required for infants, toddlers, elderly persons, and others on limited diets.

"Whenever possible, choose cans and jars in sizes that will fill your family's needs for only one meal. This is especially desirable for meat, poultry, fish, vegetables, evaporated milk, and other foods that deteriorate rapidly after a container is opened.

SAMPLE MEAL PLANS: *No Cooking Facilities*

First day	Second day	Third day
MORNING		
Citrus fruit juice.[1] Ready-to-eat cereal. Milk, cold coffee,[2] or tea.[2] Crackers. Peanut butter or other spread.	Fruit juice.[1] Corned beef hash.[1] Crackers. Spread. Milk, cold coffee,[2] or tea.[2]	Grapefruit segments.[1] Ready-to-eat cereal. Vienna sausage.[1] Milk, cold coffee,[2] or tea.[2]
NOON		
Spaghetti with meat sauce.[1] Green beans.[1] Crackers. Spread. Milk, cold coffee,[2] or tea.[2]	Baked beans.[1] Brown bread.[1] Tomatoes.[1] Fruit.[1] Milk, cold coffee,[2] or tea.[2]	Chile con carne with beans.[1] Crackers. Fruit.[1] Cookies. Milk, cold coffee,[2] or tea.[2]

By the late 1950s, surviving the deadly effects of radioactive fallout became the primary focus of the nation's civil defense efforts. The ever-expanding destructive power of hydrogen bombs meant more intense and greater reach of fallout. If you rode the city bus, you saw posters warning about fallout and encouragement to learn more about how survive its effects. By the early 1960s, after President John Kennedy introduced the community shelter program, yellow signs indicating the location of fallout shelters began to appear on office buildings, schools, and other public facilities. And magazines began to publish cover stories on the danger of fallout and ways to combat it.

In 1958, the Office of Civil and Defense Mobilization (OCDM) addressed the issue in *Facts About Fallout Protection*, a small pamphlet that summarized in simple-to-understand language what fallout is and what to do in order to survive.

"Fallout is tiny pieces of dust and debris," it read, "which are made radioactive by nuclear explosions. When a hydrogen bomb is exploded close to the ground, thousands of tons of these tiny particles of dust and debris are sucked upward high into the air. They help form the mushroom cloud which is always seen with one of these explosions.

"Some of this radioactive matter spills out of the cloud near the explosion. Most of it is carried by the wind for many miles. Eventually it settles to earth. It is called fallout and continues to give off radioactivity until it decays."

To ease people's anxiety and fear about radioactivity, the pamphlet emphasized that although "the whole world is radioactive . . . normal amounts of it are not dangerous. Only when radioactivity is present in large amounts does it become dangerous."

Then, reintroducing anxiety and fear, the pamphlet stressed that hydrogen bomb explosions create large amounts of radioactive fallout that could reach every part of the country. Moreover, because you can't feel or see fallout, being exposed to it more than likely would result in serious illness and even death.

By the early 1960s, these signs indicating the location of fallout shelters became commonplace in city downtown areas.

"A mass of materials between you and the particles is needed for protection. Weather and radiological experts will estimate the path and speed of fallout after an attack. They will tell you how much time you have to protect yourself. If you don't get the word, play it safe. Seek the best available shelter if there has been a nuclear attack.

"Your CONELRAD radio stations, at 640 or 1240 on your dial, will keep you informed.

"Radiological monitors will measure the amount of fallout in your area. Local officials will tell you when the area is safe and when you may leave the protected area.

"But the basic responsibility is yours. Listen for the instructions of your local officials. Follow them carefully."

The pamphlet contained advice on various types of shelters or shelter areas in the house, with an emphasis on being prepared:

Beginning in the late 1950s, city buses displayed these civil defense posters about radioactive fallout; and magazines, such as *Life*, featured cover stories on how to survive radioactive fallout.

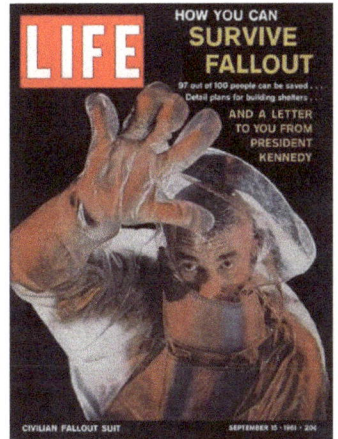

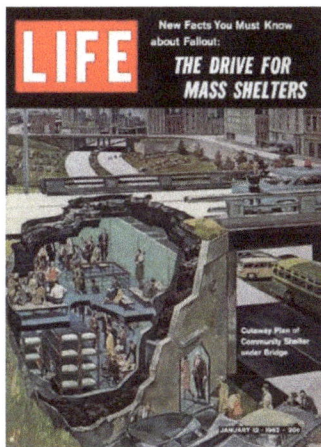

"Fallout will sift into your house or shelter like dust. Stop up the doors and windows tightly. If you think you have been in a fallout area, wash yourself and your clothes thoroughly. If you can't wash your clothes ... leave your clothes outside."

The pamphlet ended with the "Five Steps to Safety": Warning signals; your community plan for emergency action; protection from radioactive fallout; home emergency preparedness; and use of CONELRAD—640 or 1240—for official directions.

S.C. Johnson & Son, Inc. (Johnson's Wax), headquartered in Racine, Wisconsin, was one of many companies throughout the nation that published civil defense pamphlets for their employees. In 1959, the company published *Civil Defense Information for Your Family*, a 12-page booklet containing the basic elements for surviving a nuclear attack: learning the warning signals, preparing a family shelter, and stockpiling an adequate food and water supply. It also recommended creating a "family action plan" by assigning each member an emergency responsibility. "The family may be separated before an attack. It may be safer for you to remain at work or for children to remain at school. Plan to meet later at a pre-selected meeting place, but only when it is safe to move about."

The booklet began with a warning message from Howard Packard, company president: "In today's troubled world, alert men and women must realistically face the possi-bility of a surprise H-bomb attack. In the catastrophe of an all-out war, radioactive fallout would contaminate nearly every portion of this nation. H-bomb and missile blast patterns would devastate widespread areas.

"YOUR SURVIVAL in a nuclear attack depends mainly on *YOU*.

"NOW is the time for you and your family to *inform* yourselves, make emergency plans, and learn to work together as a *team*.

"From the many detailed pamphlets and publications issued by the Civilian Defense Organization, the following summary of key survival tips has been prepared for Johnson's Wax employees and their families:

"We hope and believe there will be no war, yet the risk is ever present and we don't know what the future may bring."

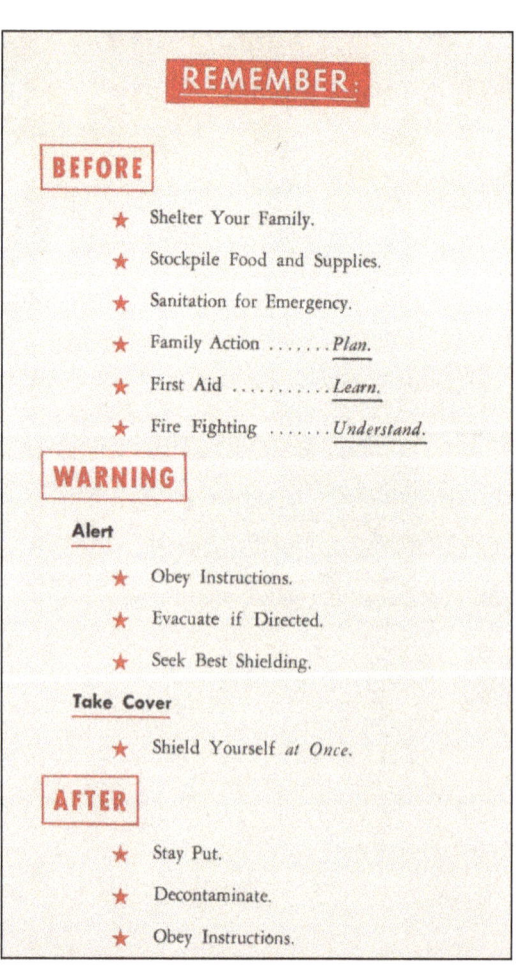

REMEMBER:

BEFORE
★ Shelter Your Family.
★ Stockpile Food and Supplies.
★ Sanitation for Emergency.
★ Family Action .... *Plan.*
★ First Aid .... *Learn.*
★ Fire Fighting .... *Understand.*

WARNING
Alert
★ Obey Instructions.
★ Evacuate if Directed.
★ Seek Best Shielding.

Take Cover
★ Shield Yourself *at Once.*

AFTER
★ Stay Put.
★ Decontaminate.
★ Obey Instructions.

The Atom Bomb Appears First As a Ball of Fire

An illustration often reproduced in civil defense publications.

In August 1961, *The Evening Sun* newspaper in Baltimore, Maryland, ran a series of articles by *Sun* writer John D. Hackett on civil defense, and published a 32-page booklet based on the series titled *If An Attack Comes*. Hackett opened the booklet with a short essay titled "Civil Defense: Your Life Easily May Depend on How Well You Are Prepared" that ended with a life-or-death question:

"Baltimore is a 'critical target' for an enemy bomb. It is the sixth largest United States city, a principal railroad hub with the fourth largest ocean port. The largest single steel mill, a major missile factory and a modern jet airport are next door. The area is a major production center for steel, copper, aluminum, chemicals, ships, missiles, electronics, automobiles, apparel, food and research. Some 939,000 people live in Baltimore. You are one of them.

"If the enemy dropped an H-bomb in this area right now—could you come out alive?"

The booklet included how to prepare for an attack, what to do when an attack happens, and, most important, the steps to survive an attack.

"What you learn now may save your life later," it read. "You must understand the power of an H-bomb blast, the dangers of its radioactive fallout, survival plans and what to do if a thermonuclear attack should come."

It then reminded readers about being prepared for the possibility of another type of war, such as gas, germs, and conventional bombs.

"What if nations agree not to use their atomic weapons and the United States becomes involved in a conventional-type war? Or, other types of warfare are used?

"You must know how to protect yourself against these weapons as well as the H-Bomb and radioactive fallout."

An example of the many posters issued by the Federal Civil Defense Administration.

The Rural Civil Defense Youth Program

OFFICE OF CIVIL AND DEFENSE MOBILIZATION

The Office of Civil and Defense Mobilization introduced the Rural Civil Defense Youth Program in the late 1950s to encourage rural youth to be "better citizens in tomorrow's world by doing their share now in America's civil defense mission." The OCDM published a *Leader's Guide* containing the objectives of the program, sample youth group activities and projects, and guidelines for a leader's preparation.

"This Guide is for you who lead and teach American boys and girls. Civil Defense is based on the first law of nature—self-preservation. It is needed and can be had by every family, in every home, everywhere. First, and young people share this responsibility, people must learn what the hazards are and what protective steps to take—then take them. This program gives you the facts and helps you teach the youth you serve.

"You will learn that Civil Defense in the home, on the farm, in your community, is not difficult. It is a simple, practical program. And nothing you do could have a more positive influence on world events because through Civil Defense you become a personal and vital part of national security. You help deter war because an enemy would not attack if our people are prepared to survive; and you help assure personal as well as national survival if nuclear war should come."

The *Leader's Guide* recommended that activities should reflect the areas rural youth are more interested, ranging from radioactive fallout and attack warnings, to protecting farm animals and planning a family fallout shelter.

In planning a family fallout shelter, the guide suggested that the youth and his or her family learn about the need for a shelter, then decide their best available option for immediate use and whether new construction of a shelter is necessary to ensure their protection from radioactive fallout. A related project was for the boys and girls to interest their friends in learning more about family fallout shelters.

The message to those leading the program was clear: "Communism is the enemy of our democracy. Russia has nuclear weapons which might be used against us, and other hostile nations may soon have them. It is an age of danger, but not hopeless danger. . . .

"Civil Defense will come into being only when everyone knows what to do and is prepared to do it. This Guide suggests ways in which you and your boys and girls may work toward these aims."

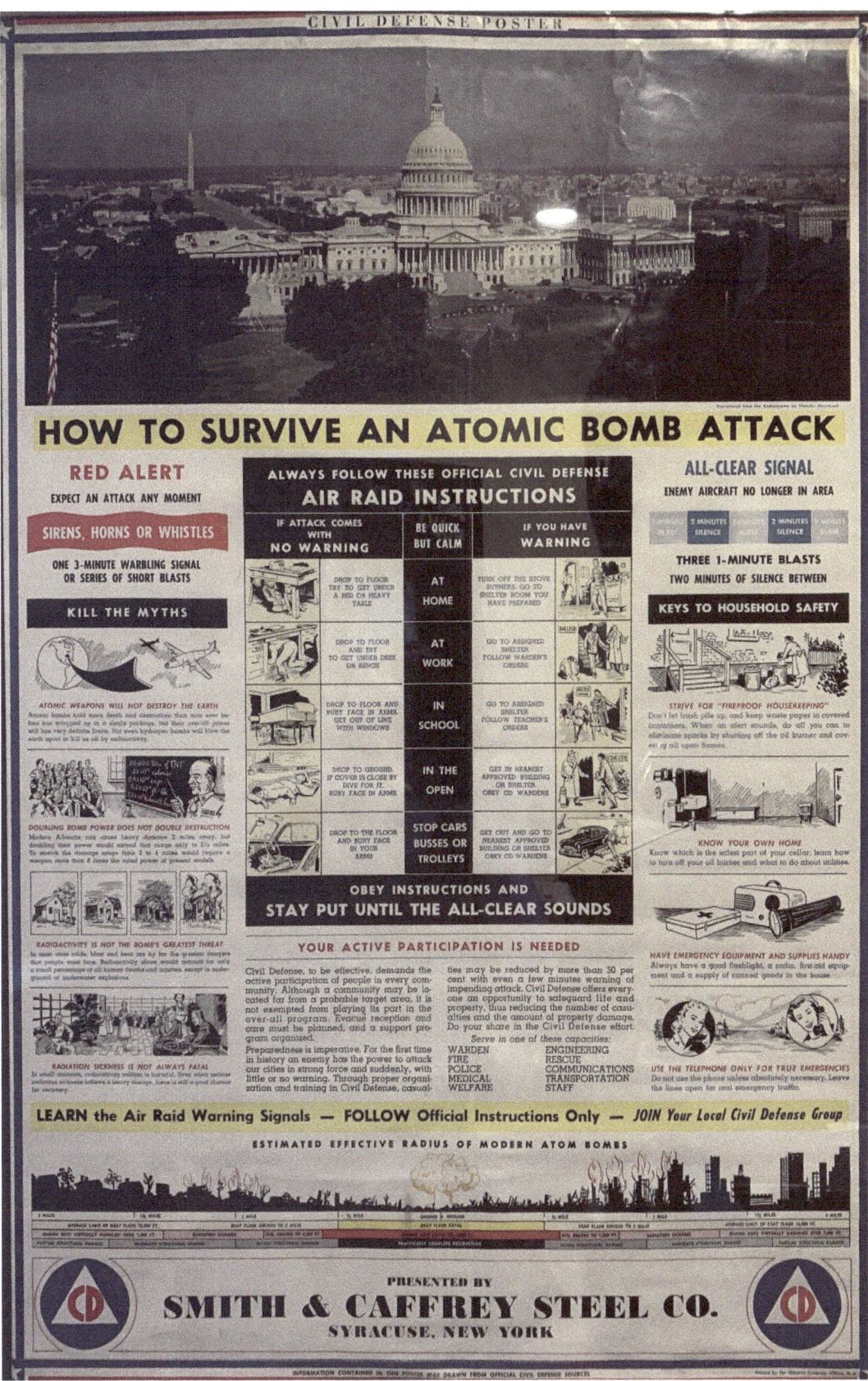

An example of the types of posters printed and distributed by private companies.

The United States introduced Operation Alert in 1954, an annual hypothetical nuclear attack that targeted major cities across the country. Cities conducted civil defense drills in conjunction with Operation Alert, including the nation's capital. President Dwight Eisenhower even participated, leaving the White House by helicopter to an unknown, protected location. The annual exercise ended in 1961.

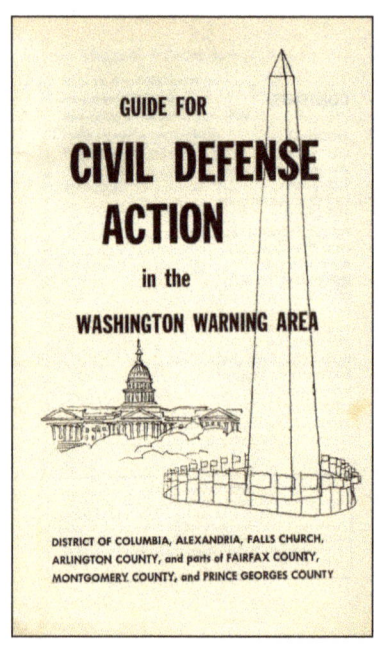

GUIDE FOR

CIVIL DEFENSE ACTION

in the

WASHINGTON WARNING AREA

DISTRICT OF COLUMBIA, ALEXANDRIA, FALLS CHURCH, ARLINGTON COUNTY, and parts of FAIRFAX COUNTY, MONTGOMERY COUNTY, and PRINCE GEORGES COUNTY

In 1959, the state governments of Maryland and Virginia, the District of Columbia, and the communities within the Washington Warning Area, in cooperation with the Office of Civil and Defense Mobilization, joined together to issue an evacuation map and civil defense instructions in *Guide for Civil Defense Action in the Washington Warning Area*. What this booklet verified was that no area, even the White House, was safe from an enemy attack.

"This booklet is your guide to action in the event of nuclear attack," the foreword read. "The better prepared the American people are to survive nuclear attack, the less chance there is that there will be war."

The booklet contained all the same information found in civil defense publications throughout the 1950s, including warning signals, radioactive fallout protection, the important of home shelters, and essential survival items. Most important, though, it explained how to use the map and what action to take.

"Determine whether you life or work in the Evacuation Zone. . . . Trace the most convenient evacuation route for you. Learn the reception area designated for people in your part of the zone. Note the difference between DAYTIME and NIGHTTIME evacuation routes. Directional street signs will mark the routes.

"Reception areas are selected counties in Maryland, Virginia, and West Virginia. A maximum effort will be made in these areas to give evacuees food, shelter, clothing, medical attention, and other necessities. It is recognized, however, that these essential items will be scarce—so YOU SHOULD TAKE SURVIVAL ITEMS WITH YOU.

"Familiarize yourself with the evacuation routes. Always keep your automobile gas tank at least half full. Keep a supply of food, water, and other essential survival items available to load in your car. Ride-sharing will be necessary in an evacuation. Motorists are urged to give rides. Trains will help in the evacuation of people who do not have cars."

THE
WHITE HOUSE
LAFAYETTE
THE
WHITE
HOUSE
PENNSYLVANIA
NEW YORK
MASSACHUSETTS
VERMONT
16TH
17TH
22ND
23RD
STREET
AVENUE
NEW
ELLIPSE
MADISON
POTOMAC RIVER
ALEXANDRIA
WASHINGTON WARNING AREA
MAP I
EVACUATION ROUTES
Arrows indicate directions to go and are the same day and night except between the two D.C Blue boundaries.
OPEN AND CLOSED DASHED LINES ARE THE EVACUATION BOUNDARIES
This boundary is the same day or night
D.C. night boundary in effect 6:30 p.m. to 7:30 a.m. durin these hours people south of this line move out to the south.
D.C. day boundary in effect 7:30 a.m to 6:30 p.m. during these hours people north of this line move out to the north.
This shows 2-way traffic for Civil Defense vehicles. 2-way blue arrow routes are in effect only at the times the associated blue boundary is in effect.
Railroad passenger loading points
U.S. ROUTES
STATE ROUTES
Graphic Scale in Miles
MILES

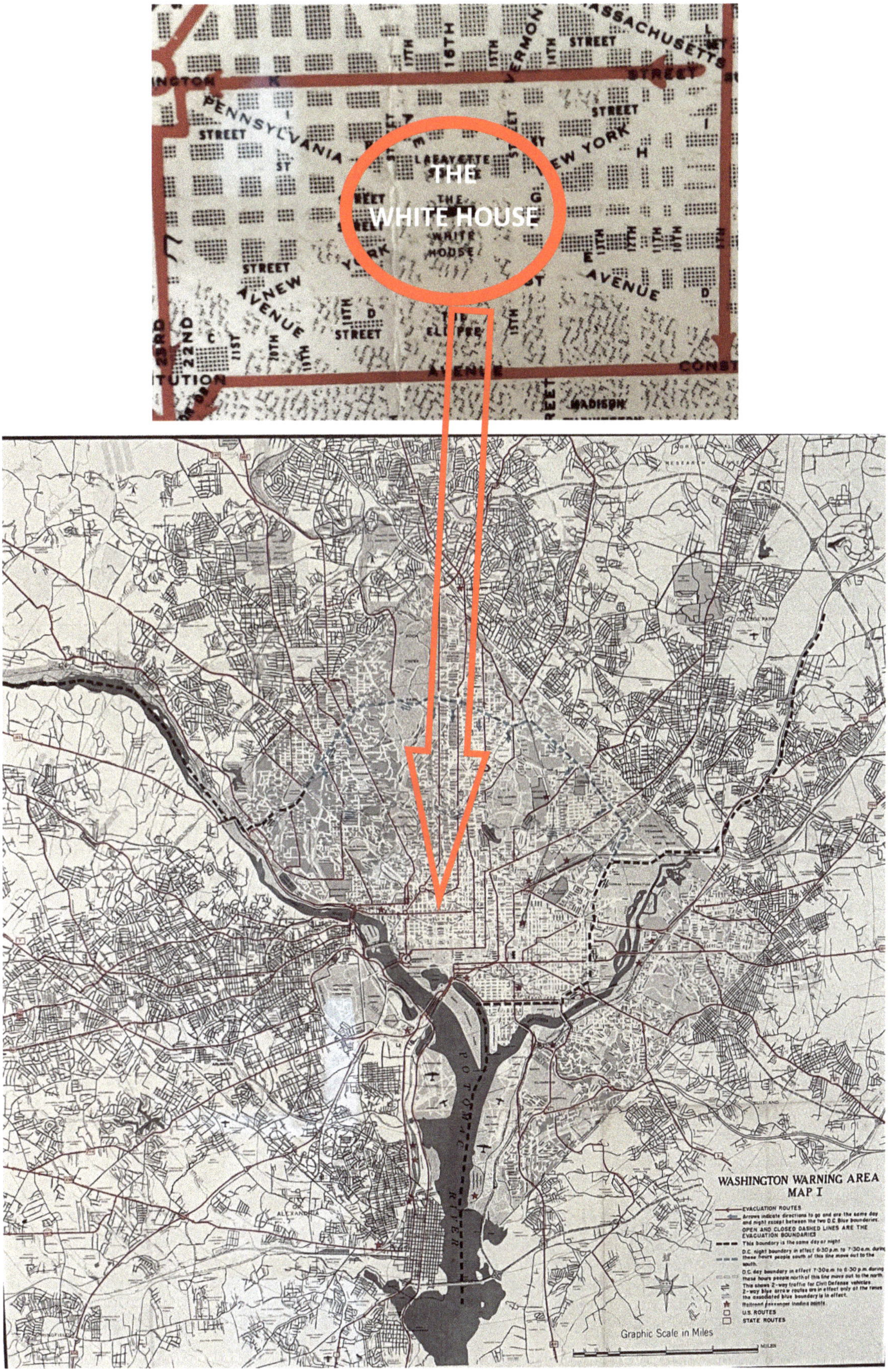

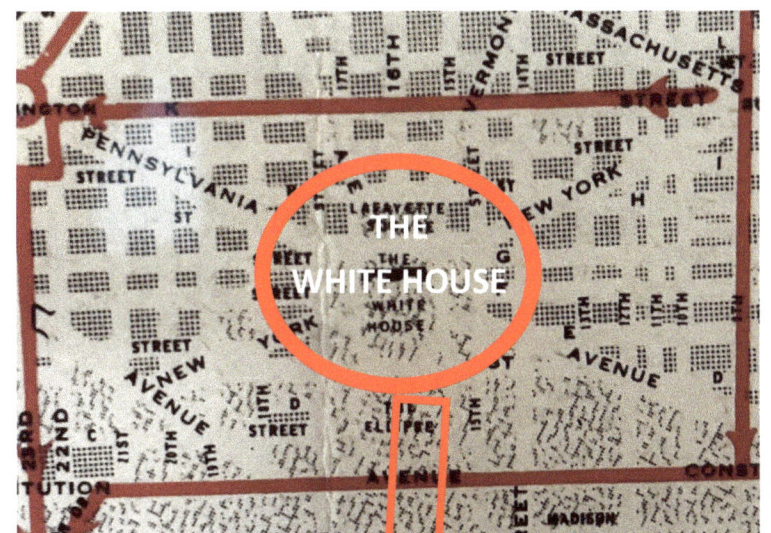

Conclusion: A Continuing Threat

"The primary objective of civil defense, survival of our people in the event of nuclear war, is of utmost importance to our government and to every person in the United States. Protection of our population should be the basic concern of every American. . . . The time is becoming urgent and unless each of us prepares now, our freedom of choice could very well slip from our grasp."

Those were the words of President John Kennedy at a meeting of civil defense officials. With Kennedy's support, civil defense efforts continued into the 1960s. In September 1961, the government replaced President Eisenhower's National Plan for Civil and Defense Mobilization, which merely encouraged the building of family fallout shelters, by launching the Community Fallout Shelter Program. Commenting on the program, President Kennedy emphasized that those not hit directly in a nuclear blast can be saved "if they can be warned to take shelter and if that shelter is available."

Civil defense was not the only government program continuing; so were tests of nuclear weapons. Between 1945 and 1960, the United States conducted 194 nuclear tests. Then, as Kennedy's "New Frontier" got underway, radioactive deposits were found in wheat and milk in several states, triggering a new alarm about the dangers of atomic bomb tests. The Soviet Union, however, not only continued its atmospheric tests, it expanded them. In 1961, it detonated 31 nuclear bombs over a three-month period—the largest bomb being 58 megatons, or 4,000 times more powerful than the atomic bomb dropped on Hiroshima, Japan, on August 6, 1945.

Kennedy had supported a ban on testing since 1956; and when elected president in 1960, he pledged to work toward a nuclear test ban treaty and made stopping nuclear tests a priority, but without success. After failing to respond immediately to the Soviet Union's expansion of its testing program, he finally renewed the nation's testing program in April 1962. Then, a year later, in June 1963, he announced that the United States and the Soviet Union would soon begin a new round of negotiations on an agreement to end testing. A month later, after 12 days of negotiations, the two countries agreed to ban nuclear tests in the atmosphere, under water, and in space. Both nations signed the Limited Test Ban Treaty on August 5, 1963; the Senate approved the treaty on September 23; and President Kennedy signed it on October 7—six weeks before his assassination in Dallas, Texas, on November 22, 1963.

The following year, on October 16, 1964, the People's Republic of China exploded its first nuclear bomb, creating yet another threat to world peace and ending hopes of an end to the Cold War.

As the 1960s unfolded, the nation's focus slowly turned toward more immediate problems: the civil rights movement, the Vietnam War, and student protests. Yet civil defense efforts continued.

Your Family Survival Plan, published in 1965 by the Office of Civil Defense, which had replaced the Office of Civil and Defense Mobilization, in cooperation with the Federal Extension Service of the U.S. Department of Agriculture, provided updated instructions on how to prepare for—and survive—an enemy attack:

"How well are you prepared to meet an emergency?" it asked. "Over the years families take various steps for protection and security. You carry fire insurance on your home, auto insurance, health insurance. Why? Just in case something happens. These protective steps fit into your plan for living.

"Your family also needs a protective plan for survival—another kind of insurance 'just in case' of fallout from nuclear attack."

More than a decade later, in 1977, the Defense Civil Preparedness Agency in the Department of Defense published *Protection in the Nuclear Age* with a message that has proved to be prophetic about today's state of the world:

"In this uneasy age in which we live, strife abounds in many troubled parts of the world. The weapons of modern warfare have become increasingly powerful and numerous. Potential aggressors can deliver nuclear warheads accurately on targets up to 8,000 miles away. Despite continuing efforts to achieve and maintain peace, a nuclear attack upon the United States remains a distinct possibility."

www.ingramcontent.com/pod-product-compliance
Lightning Source LLC
Chambersburg PA
CBHW042208300626
47475CB00043B/525